Becoming Adept

Applying Leadership Strategies For Lasting Change

Paul DePalma

Mira Kacee Press

Published by Mira Kacee Press

ISBN: 978-0-9989874-0-8

Typesetting services by BOOKOW.COM

To my father who always supported me,
but never saw this coming

Preface

"The price of success is hard work, dedication to the job at hand, and the determination that whether we win or lose, we have applied the best of ourselves to the task at hand." ~ Vince Lombardi

Adept. It is a word you have certainly heard, but probably don't use regularly. You may not even know its dictionary definition. The act of becoming adept is simply growing to be very skilled or proficient at something. That something could be anything. It could be developing into a skilled chef, a strong writer, an accomplished athlete, or for purposes of our journey, a great leader.

This book is offered as a practical guide for improving individuals, teams, and organizations from an observer of effective and ineffective leadership behaviors. It is not an academic study. This book doesn't contain reams of hard data, nor does it provide the level of rigor you would find around exhaustive research studies on the topics of leadership, management and organization development. Although I graduated with a degree in Economics from Boston College and have a Master's Degree in Organization Development from Bowling Green State University, I have not devoted my life to extensive academic research in the field of OD.

However, I do have significant experience. I've had my own leadership opportunities in interviewing, hiring, training and sometimes firing people when there wasn't a fit or I made a mistake. I've owned a handful of different businesses and I've signed both sides of a pay-check. Additionally, as of this writing, I estimate that I've walked through the doors of well over a thousand unique organization lo-cations. In small groups of rarely more than 14 people, I've worked closely with thousands of people over the years to help them be more effective. This process has provided me with an opportunity to wit-ness countless different individual perspectives and numerous group cultures along the way.

It's been 27 years since I left a very promising career in pharmaceu-tical sales to enter the world of consulting and organization develop-ment. As opposed to most people in my field, I didn't work for a lot of years in a large corporation, leave to develop my own consul-tancy, and then proceed to tell everyone the techniques and methods I had used during my corporate career. Instead, I jumped right in and started my business at a young age and have learned over the years from my clients and the results they've produced, the key elements of productivity, management, and leadership effectiveness that can make the biggest impact. I believe this gives me a unique perspective, instead of coming into my client work with preconceived notions and rigid biases, I have learned by seeing what works through trial and er-ror, insight and action, cause and effect. What that provides for you is reassurance that the ideas presented here are time tested, and that the tactics suggested are both proven and extend beyond just my own personal behavior and practice.

To date, I have not conducted scientific research on the theories I present in this book. But I have the data, and maybe that's another book! What I do offer is the informal research I conduct daily by being keenly observant, diligently persistent and asking a ton of ques-tions. As a practitioner of a craft working with organizations large and small to improve their results, this book is not only about those organizations and people that I've seen grow and prosper, but about my own journey of steady, sustained, incremental improvement in learning from them and applying what works.

What I've realized is that the concept of incremental improvement really works. I believe that this book will help you, both as a leader, and as a member of the team, to become more adept at applying the improvements to reap big benefits. It is not technology, nor fancy algorithms, nor dangling carrots that improve business practices. It is people. There is nothing in the world that can change human behavior more effectively than the choices and actions of humans themselves.

One of the biggest realizations for me has been that the difference between a successful organization and one that is not successful is their people's ability to change and adapt. It's amazing to me that many leaders believe they can just "put the right people on the bus" and expect sustainable results from them, without any further investment in their development. Thinking like that short changes individual growth, and doesn't respect the idea that a person is a living, growing being that is nowhere near living up to their true potential. Investing in their people and fostering their growth can have the biggest impact on organization success and is a key differentiator between successful companies and their less successful competitors. I want to inspire you to see that your organization should be doing this. Not just one time, not just through a program, but constantly, relentlessly.

I believe that we spend far too much time trying to provide information to people and not enough time increasing the capability of people to use and apply information to make a difference. This book will take a creative and unique look at helping leaders understand how to bring out the potential in themselves and others, encourage those that struggle with change, and provide the inspiration they need to make an impact on the world as a whole.

Within each of us lies the ability to become adept. We share a common thread of desire to develop, grow, and be highly regarded in our respective careers. Together in these pages, we will work to transition and transform into the best version of ourselves. Now it is time to take action toward liberating our true potential.

Acknowledgments

For me, writing a book has been like working on a major home improvement project. You're sometimes really focused, making great progress. And other times it feels more haphazard, you do a little here, a little there. Sometimes things fall into place and move quickly while at other times it seems like you're going backward and you would rather hit yourself with a hammer. In the end, you are grateful that it's done and you look back and realize you could have never done it alone. The outcome of this project was the result of insight, hard work, and feedback from many other people along the way.

Thank you to John M. Ward, my former business partner, who originated the ADEPT acronym and co-authored many of the training programs that are the basis of what is now known as ADEPT Leadership. ADEPT could not have come to life without his efforts and collaboration.

Thank you, Harlan Kickhoefer, Jenny Riggs, Brian McCann, Salim Kouidri, Jennifer Donohue, Pat Brown, Roger Oxendale, Al Frangipane, Will Smith, Paul Upshaw, Derek Thomas and Alex Moore for sharing your comments and stories, some of which I've used in this book. And thank you to Brie Okkerse, Dave Griffin, Matt Kibbey, Roland Loup, Tim Bryant, Will Hill and Mallory Curtis for reading the early manuscripts and providing valuable feedback. I am truly grateful.

To Justin Spizman, the "Georgia Author of the Year" and a great book architect. He kept me on task during the writing of this book, showed never ending patience, and provided a kick in the pants when I needed it. To Joby Burrows, a talented editor and insightful collaborator who also happens to be a fantastic big sister. Many thanks to my brothers, Dave DePalma, a lifetime source of positive support and encouragement, and John DePalma whose thoughtfulness opens my mind to things I might not have considered. And to my friend Dave McLaughlin, for navigating early versions of this book and always providing a thorough analysis. They have all contributed ideas that helped make my crude attempts into a more functional effort.

I want to thank Tania Rodriguez-Severance, my long-time business assistant and Director of Client Services at ADEPT Leadership. I appreciate her always watching my back, taking ownership for how we appear to the world, and for her loyalty through thick and thin over the last 13 years.

Special thanks to Dr. Diana Wong, my former professor, coach, critical supporter, and good friend. Her enthusiasm and encouragement have been an inspiration. And to Sam Maitz, a key influencer in my early consulting career, who lives the habits of incremental improvement and has made it his habit to call me on my birthday every year.

I want to thank my mother, Cee, for being one of my best friends and a constant source of clarity on issues, unlimited inspiration, and unconditional love.

Finally, I'd like to thank my daughter Jenna for all she's taught me throughout her young life, and my wife Tess who supported me behind the scenes even before she knew what the book was about, and later took a more active role in helping craft a better story and more impactful book. I'm so grateful for their love and support.

Contents

Chapter 1- Perspective

The Importance of Incremental Improvement

Pablo Picasso said, "Action is the foundational key to all success." In each of us lies an undeniable passion and fire to go beyond the ordinary. We all hope to reach high and even higher. Whatever the measuring stick may be, we want to exceed its height. For many of us, the journey isn't a straight shot but a walk along many long and winding roads. Each of these journeys is comprised of thousands of steps, or marginal gains, that position us closer to the exact coordinates we strive to locate. Although the road to success is paved with these incremental gains, without action, success is nothing more than a hope or dream.

One Inch at a Time

"It's a game of inches."

As a sports fan, I've heard that phrase all my life. I can't even tell you which sport originated the term - every sport seems to take credit for it. A NASCAR race can be decided by just one millimeter, a swim meet by the tip of a finger, a baseball game by a ball falling short at the warning track, a golf game by the putt that lips out of the hole, or in football, a winning field goal attempt that glances off the upright and falls to the ground. In each of these examples, mere inches were the difference between victory and defeat.

Often, it seems that a single dramatic event decides the outcome of an entire game, as if a supernatural force had intervened like a lightning bolt. The timing of the circumstances magnifies the value of that event, or in other words, that inch. But anyone involved in those competitions will often say that it didn't really come down to just that inch. That inch may be the pivotal moment, but many inches led to a dramatic conclusion. Other moments or inches during the game could have made that final moment unnecessary and insignificant if they had gone the other way. In reality, these events are the culmination of a "game of inches." Although it appears a contest was won or lost on a last inch, the sum of inches over time truly led to the final outcome.

In life, as in sports, the game of inches is an accumulation of incremental steps. In sports, the real game of inches is in the attempt to locate those small adjustments that produce better results. A baseball batter practices his swing over and over to perfect his stroke so he can bring it to the game every night. Slight changes can produce a small difference in outcomes, which can have a huge impact on overall results. If a batter has just one more hit every ten at bats (a .200 verses a .300 batting average), it's often the difference between losing a job and being demoted rather than making millions of dollars as an All-Star player.

In 1992, Major League Baseball teams drafted Phil Nevin and Derek Jeter. Nevin was the overall number one pick, five spots before Jeter at number six. Nevin played for twelve years and accumulated a .270 batting average. Jeter played for twenty years with a .310 batting average. Nevin's career was average, whereas Jeter was a perennial All-Star, World Series Most Valuable Player, and a first-ballot Hall of Famer. Their batting averages differed by less than half of one hit for every ten at bats. While this signified a small difference in their overall performance, it had an enormous impact on the game and the overall legacy of each player.[1]

Incremental Change

In systems all around us, numerous examples of the power of incremental improvements abound. In nature, a tree grows slowly from a seedling and over decades can become a mighty oak. The slow growth leads to tremendous strength. Species of trees such as laurel oaks that were bred to grow faster are not as strong and are much more susceptible to disease than their live oak cousins, which can withstand the ravages of nature and live for up to three hundred years. The point of this example: It takes repetition, day in and day out, to reach your goals and show substantial improvement and growth.

The laws of incremental change cannot be short-circuited. There are no shortcuts. A person cannot learn a new language without time and practice. It takes repetitious memorization to simply learn the words you need before you can apply new rules of grammar and spelling. You can't play an instrument just by reading a book. And although technology has dramatically changed surgical procedures and the practice of medicine, it still takes about nine months to produce a baby.

The ancient art of bonsai demonstrates incremental improvement in its most tedious form. Although legend suggests the art form may date back to the Han Dynasty (between 206 BC and AD 220), hard evidence shows it was active in the Tan Dynasty, some thirteen hundred years ago. In bonsai, plants and trees are continuously pruned

---

[1] Barron, David. "Phil Nevin, the player the Astros took ahead of Derek Jeter, has no regrets." Houston Chronicle. April 01, 2014. Accessed May 01, 2017. http://www.houstonchronicle.com/sports/astros/article/Phil-Nevin-the-player-the-Astros-took-ahead-of-5367655.php.

and trimmed to an amazingly small size, but they mimic the look of a full-grown tree. Many imposter starter trees exist, but a true bonsai takes years, even decades, to grow to full strength and beauty.[2]

Bonsais are highly valued. One sold for $1.3 million - the highest price ever paid for a bonsai - in Takamatsu, Japan. This centuries-old pine tree has been cultivated for generations. Think about the discipline, focus, and daily diligence it takes to nurture such a wonderful and incremental miracle of nature. Many of us can barely keep a potted plant we received as a gift alive long enough to put it into the ground. So, imagine watering, pruning, and managing the environment of a bonsai for decades longer than most people raise their children. Bonsai may not be your cup of tea, but you cannot deny the dedication required to create these living works of art. Inch by inch, day by day, step by step, and delicate snip by snip, they come to life.

Bonsai illustrates yet another element of incremental improvement. Although the magnificent plant is a wonderful demonstration of the hard work of the master, most masters will tell you that the real outcome is how the work itself *developed the master*. Beyond producing a desired outcome, incremental improvement brings value to the people who participate in it. That is, discipline, dedication, and outright hard work turn a novice into an expert.

Each of these examples demonstrates many of the same principles and fundamental concepts governing organizations and businesses. Understanding the laws of incremental improvement helps us understand how growth occurs. Small things done well impact the culture of the organization. Over time, those small things lead to results, performance outcomes, and ultimately, high levels of success. In attempting to lead others, trial, error, action, and outcomes help the

---

[2] KLDesigns. "History of Bonsai." History of Bonsai. Accessed May 01, 2017. http://www.celestialbonsai.com/history.html.

individual grow and develop. These incremental changes, or organizational inches, are not mysteries; they are represented by the fundamentals that are practiced by leaders and employees throughout the organization.

Like the poker player who studies each of his opponents for behavioral clues or tells that can provide insight into their next move, academics and practitioners alike have studied organizations and how they work and have observed many organizational tells of success that are proven to produce results. The majority of them can be practiced by anyone.

Pretty exciting, isn't it?

The Quick Fix

Somehow, we easily forget the laws of incremental improvement. Our popular culture is always touting the quick wins, the meteoric rise of a business, and dramatic growth. We are enthralled with stories about companies that achieved success almost overnight.

Kevin Systrom and Mike Krieger founded Instagram, a photo sharing application for smartphones, in October 2010. In just two months, it reached over one million users. In December 2011, people voted it the "iPhone App of the Year." Less than two years after its founding, Facebook bought the company for a billion dollars. ONE BILLION.[3] Overnight, the company's worth exceeded that of the *New York Times*, a multimedia conglomerate founded in 1851 and at the forefront of written media for more than one hundred fifty years. A less than two-year-old startup had overtaken a media giant that had been in business for more than fifteen decades and had more than three thousand employees.

---

[3] Rusli, Evelyn M. "Facebook Buys Instagram for $1 Billion." The New York Times. April 09, 2012. Accessed May 01, 2017. https://dealbook.nytimes.com/2012/04/09/facebook-buys-instagram-for-1-billion/?_r=0.

Stories like this promote our dreams of the quick fix and our belief in a miraculous solution. The media frenzy creates a level of expectation that contradicts the fundamentals of incremental growth. News stories and social media make entrepreneurs tense. They begin to believe they need to be immediately viable and must achieve soaring growth. If they do not take off like a rocket ship, they feel as though they are falling to the bottom of the sea like an anchor. This belief system persuades us to believe we are doing something wrong if we aren't skyrocketing to success. It sometimes encourages the wrong types of leadership behavior, promotes short-term solutions, band-aid approaches, and kicking the can down the road with the faulty hope and aspiration of better results.

Setting out to achieve this kind of success is equivalent to taking your money and putting it all on black at the roulette wheel, or using all of your savings to play the lottery. Yes, you do have a chance of winning and winning big. However, the majority lose and squander their time, energy, and resources in pursuit of something that requires outside forces or a once-in-a-lifetime opportunity to obtain. The odds simply are not in your favor. Although many people dream of creating the next Instagram, the chances of that happening are probably the same as getting struck by lightning while you're being attacked by a shark: extremely slim - even if you can find the shark during a storm.

Simple Isn't Easy

The incremental laws are also forgotten because although simple, they are not easy. Frank Bettger, in his legendary book *How I Raised Myself from Failure to Success in Selling*, speaks to this conundrum. He says people often try to shortcut simple things. They get lazy and try to outthink the process they know works because that process is not easy. In sales that means not making the calls, not building the relationships, and not doing the work. He goes on to say that "sales can be easy if you work it hard, but hard if you work it easy." When you don't make your calls, when you don't fill out your reports, and when you talk yourself out of making that late meeting, you are making the process of getting results more difficult to achieve than if you did the work thoroughly and diligently. The same is true of the incremental laws. They can be hard, they can be challenging to achieve, and the result is that some people just stop trying before they even fail. If leadership was easy, everyone would be successful at it.

Humans try to find shortcuts all the time - it's part of our constitution. We are trained to want things now. Our lives are filled with instant gratification. Sometimes this leads to new processes and procedures. However, when we're talking about people change, we're talking about ingrained habits and actions that aren't easily changed. With these, there is no quick fix.

Warren Buffett, one of the wealthiest men in the world, has made his money incrementally. No one can point to just one deal that made the man a financial legend. Moreover, his character and habits produced his wealth and have sustained it dramatically over the years. Buffett's actions and behaviors over time speak strongly to the power of incremental improvement. Leaders can learn much from him.

When you think about incremental improvement, consider that:

- *Inches can be taken slowly and accumulated over time.*

- *A small change conducted incrementally can make a huge difference.*

- *Incremental improvement is powerful and sustainable.*

- *Incremental improvement impacts the outcome and the individual involved in the process.*

7

- *Real personal growth and organizational leadership are about making changes in action and behavior to produce better results.*

Unfortunately, often we minimize the impact of small changes. We strive to hit home runs and frequently slough off the singles as less worthwhile or even insignificant. We have a habit of viewing change as immediately insignificant. For example, recently a client told me he was organizing his day in a way that was helpful but "only worth" about ten minutes a day in real gains. Well at work, ten minutes a day becomes fifty minutes per week. In a year, that equates to a forty-hour work week of saved time. If employees were told they would receive an extra week of vacation if they could increase their productivity by only ten minutes per day, do you think there would be a lot of interest? Often, managers don't look at the power of incremental improvement because they are shortsighted about its impact. Gaining inches is a golden opportunity for unbelievable improvement in the long run.

Sadly, we seem to be shortsighted about change. Maybe it's because it takes patience. Maybe it's because we can't seem to see beyond the next couple of hours, never mind considering tomorrow or next week. Or maybe it is because we can survive without changing, even though we may not evolve, prosper, or develop at high levels.

Breaking Habits to Create Change

In making organizational change, leaders are challenged by the speed with which individuals can consider new ideas and implement new habits. Habits are ingrained in people. The most deeply ingrained ones are our personal beliefs. These mental pillars can slow the process of change as individuals reconcile changes with the way they are currently thinking. The more strongly held thoughts and beliefs are, the bigger the obstacle of considering a new way of doing things. Often, these habits result from years of doing things the same way, believing in things in the same manner, and recognizing that it is easier to let your subconscious steer the ship. When you begin the process of breaking these habits, a manager can experience delegation that backfires, resulting in a poor outcome. This result creates a desire to quickly revert to the old behavior, and the resistance to delegation becomes self-fulfilling.

Once you accept the new idea, you're faced with the challenge of changing to the new behavior. Frustration can ensue when those behaviors are challenging to apply in day-to-day experiences. Over time, frustration will justify the individual to revert to the old behavior. Once that happens, the lack of progress can reinforce the previous habit of thought against doing things differently. It can cement that thought and effectively squelch the change and maybe even attempts to make similar changes in the future. When slow change doesn't produce immediate results, bad habits creep back in and cause us to take two steps in the wrong direction.

When leaders complain that "there's resistance to change and no one is getting on board," they need to realize this is a natural and perfectly reasonable response to the way they've tried to implement the change.

Let's consider this example: An organization discovers that a call center procedure for capturing specific customer data doesn't provide the right information for scheduling services and planning resources. So, a group of managers work for weeks to create a new procedure. Finally satisfied with their creation, they roll it out to the front-line organization. Unfortunately, when it's used in the call center, agents feel like it's difficult and impractical. They wonder why they weren't involved in the design of the form since they are the ones who use it every day. Does this sound familiar? Has this happened in your organization? The way people respond to change isn't a mystery. The real mystery is that organizations so frequently violate these principles of incremental improvement and are surprised when they don't work out.

Locating the Inches

So, armed with the knowledge that success, at any level, is often the culmination of a series of wins or inches, where do these inches reside? For example, in football, an inch can be found in the timing of the wide receiver's pass route. To ensure optimal performance, it is common for the quarterback to spend endless time with his receivers to repeatedly run these route patterns for hours on end until the timing is ingrained into each of them. The number of steps, the speed of those steps, and the precision of the turn all impact the success of the pattern when it's run at game speed. Any one inch can be the difference between a game-winning touchdown and a game-losing interception.

In our personal lives, incremental improvement inches are all around us for the taking. Planning before acting, inch by inch, almost always produces big results. For example, planning your meals at home gives you time to find all the necessary components and means you can pick up fresh ingredients. This can increase the pleasure of the meal, improve its overall health benefits, lead to less stress in meal preparation, and more satisfaction with the food and the budget. These benefits can help you create a more manageable weight, and your overall well-being can increase. More energy, a better attitude, and more confidence personally and professionally often result. And it started with a simple adjustment in the planning of the meal.

As you can see, taking advantage of the inches in our personal lives can lead to a better life. On the flip side, if we don't take advantage of them, we pay a price.

When we're too tired to walk for twenty minutes after work, we lose out on progress toward long-term health. When we're too busy on our smartphone to answer a question from our child, we create a little hurt and a small dent in our future relationship. When we don't help someone in need, we can miss out on benefitting them and feeling good about ourselves.

Just like in personal life, inches are abundant in work organizations. Defining an impactful vision and mission can capture the imagination of employees, while communicating the priority of objectives can increase their focus. Clarifying goals can improve motivation, and providing feedback can enhance performance. Inches are found in the efficiency of managing time and energy, in the effectiveness of communication, in the investment in development of knowledge and understanding, and in the attitudes and actions of leaders and managers. It doesn't matter in what direction or at what level you are looking, inches are there.

Principles in Practice

Many of these incremental improvements are comprised of foundational principles. A principle is a natural law or universal truth. Like gravity, principles are undeniable in their impact. The study of organizations has occurred long enough for us to understand that many organizational principles produce predictable results. Examples like planning, setting goals, collaborating, and getting people involved in change are all principles we know work effectively. However, although we may remain aware of these opportunities, we may not actually act upon them for reasons like:

- *We find it hard to notice the impact of very small changes. For example, has your spouse ever lost weight and you failed to notice those pounds?*

- *We get impatient waiting for the change to happen because it's natural to want immediate change and quick results.*

- *We don't appreciate the value of small investments over the long run. It's hard to stay focused on the goal when you run into obstacles today.*

- *We're distracted by the present moment. It's hard to chip away at something if we don't feel as though we're making progress.*

Understanding why we don't work to gain the inches is almost as important as the decision to secure them. As humans, we are certainly prewired. This wiring causes us to act or not act, be decisive or indecisive, and choose one path over the other. If we increase our awareness to understand why we do what we do, we can gain valuable insight into how we can do something different. For us, human nature often takes over and subconsciously pushes us in a specific direction, whether we want to go there or not. It is habit, natural, and unbeknownst to each of us. And that inadvertent action is where the inches begin to get lost.

Inches Lost

In his book *In Retrospect,* the late Robert McNamara, secretary of defense during the Kennedy administration, discusses the many challenges and complexities of the Vietnam conflict. He indicates that even though the Kennedy administration was filled with the "best and the brightest" young minds of that day, one key question was never asked. If South Vietnam fell to the North Vietnamese, it was assumed that Communism would spread throughout Southeast Asia and become a clear and present danger to the interests of the United States. McNamara went on to say that no one ever questioned that assumption, even though brilliant minds populated the cabinet. If that one assumption had been properly challenged and an accurate answer had been secured, the war might have been deemed unnecessary. That one inch could have saved years of strife and thousands of lives.

The examples are everywhere. In 1984, the Challenger disaster spurred many theorists to identify the cause of the tragedy. Over the years, many myths emerged, from the idea that the launch had been politically motivated to the idea that the government had recently banned a stronger sealant because it contained too much asbestos. However, some twenty-five year later, James Oberg, a twenty-two-year veteran of mission control operations at NASA's Johnson Space Center, wrote, "The disaster need never have happened if managers and workers had clung to known principles of safely operating on the edge of extreme hazards." No great insights came out of the long investigation into the tragedy. As Oberg said, "Nothing was learned by the disaster that hadn't already been learned." The ultimate problem: Those learnings had been forgotten or ignored. [4]

We are destined to pay the consequences when we forget or ignore the inches. It happens again and again. Many tragedies, wars, or disasters occur as the culmination, not the immediate reaction, of many of these inches. If even one inch was lost or gained, the disaster or tragedy may have been completely averted.

Companies can lose inches in many ways. A leader running late into weekly meetings can negatively impact their time and everyone else's. Their action also sends a poor message to the team and promotes the loss of inches through the disrespect for time. If a manager gives employees very vague instructions, or delivers them in a hurried, unclear way, most likely the team will produce poor quality work or have to redo things the right way. And if an employee starts their day with no plan, you can bet they'll waste a lot of time and energy.

But there lies the opportunity. If inches lost leads to poor efficiency, then inches gained offers a great occasion to achieve and succeed. Inches can have a big, positive impact either way.

[4] Oberg, James. "7 myths about the Challenger shuttle disaster." NBCNews.com. January 26, 2011. Accessed May 01, 2017. http://www.nbcnews.com/id/11031097/ns/technology_and_science-space/t/myths-about-challenger-shuttle-disaster/#.WPOcjIgrIps.

Alan Mulally, former CEO of Ford, turned around the automotive giant without a bailout from the government. Before Mulally, executive meetings at Ford were notorious for people hiding problems and sandbagging their data. Mulally insisted on two things in his weekly business plan review (BPR) meetings:

1. All data had to be verifiable so that everyone could see potential discrepancies and validate them in light of all other data.

2. Problems weren't solely the individual's but a team issue that needed to be solved.

Individuals were asked to step in and support rather than be thankful that something wasn't "their" issue. It was *not* a zero-sum game. All employees worked on the company's collective success and growth. These BPR meetings went from being a dysfunctional waste of time to a leading component of the eventual turnaround. The harmony and synchronicity created an abundance of small inches that manifested in the form of information exchange, dialogue, and solutions.[5] But not all companies are set up to secure these incremental gains.

On what seems like a daily basis, many companies squander the opportunity for gains. The wins are right in front of them, yet they turn a blind eye.

So, with that said, where do we, as leaders, lose those inches?

- **In Decisions.** *We lose inches by the choices we make. Choices are the split-second opportunities to decide between quick-fix and long-term investment. Each choice has a consequence, so the mindset we have when we enter into the choice has a significant impact. For*

---

[5] "Alan Mulally's Management Secret: Peer Accountability." Optimity Advisors. June 14, 2016. Accessed May 01, 2017. http://optimityadvisors.com/insights/blog/alan-mulallys-management-secret-peer-accountability.

example, tactical speed means we get things done quickly; however, sometimes moving quickly in the short run slows things in the long run. Strategic speed looks at a different perspective: What is going to be the systemic impact of the action over time?

- **With Priorities.** *We lose inches by drastic and unjustified changes in priority. As we inappropriately adapt to changes in organizational direction, differences in resources, and adjustments because of new leadership, we lose ground toward our objectives.*

- **Without Focus.** *We lose inches when we lose track of our goals. When we aren't clear that we are making progress down a specific path, we can become frustrated. Instead of sticking with the increments we've tried to accomplish, we swing for the fences.*

In each of these areas we lose an unprecedented number of wins. Each win could lock together with another, like a chain, to grow into a lifeline that could literally be the difference between sinking and swimming. By committing to incremental improvements and seeing the process through, individuals and organizations can realize performance that is greatly enhanced and sustainable. My goal is to show you how.

Adept in Action:

- Are you always looking for the quick fix and big win? If so, remember you can't lift one weight and suddenly be stronger. **Try this:** Target a significant event in the future (birthday, holiday, work anniversary) and focus your energy on your picture of success at that point in time. Then clarify the action steps to get there.

- Do you think about your objective before you act? Busyness is no substitute for results. **Try this:** Take a deep breath and picture what it will look like to reach that objective to make sure you're on track.

- Do you feel driven to immediate results by circumstances you feel are out of your control? **Try this:** Check in with your clients or connections to make sure you are providing the responsiveness that meets their needs and not just what you *think* they need.

- Do you always feel behind the eight ball, as if everything is due yesterday? **Try this:** List everything that you want to get done, clarify what matters most, and then tackle the things that need to be done first.

- Do you want more tips and tools? **Try this:** Bookmark our website www.adeptleadership.com/tools-and-tips-adept-booksite/ to access a growing repository of valuable resources.

Chapter 2 – Attention

The Painful Death of the Information Age

As a leader, one of the greatest places to increase your ability to incrementally improve is through communication, and more specifically, through the exchange of information. Steve Ballmer, former chief executive officer of Microsoft, said, "The number one benefit of information technology is that it empowers people to do what they want to do. It lets people learn things they didn't think they could learn before, and so in a sense it is all about potential."

Potential is a powerful characteristic, but its presence doesn't automatically equate to performance. Information is power, but the power of pure knowledge held by an individual is shrinking. Let's explore why.

The Devalued Value of Information

Historically, the transfer of information was the limiter in the availability and quality of information flow. You had to overcome obstacles just to access it. In ancient times, the requirement that one must be face to face to communicate limited the verbal transmission of information. Nonverbal cave drawings required access to a certain location. Smoke signals, signal fires, and whistles in the jungle were limited in the scope of information they represented. But the dissemination of information evolved.

The creation of paper allowed nonverbal communication to travel from place to place, but a limitation in the quality of roads and the speed with which they could be navigated limited their timeliness. Carrier pigeons increased the speed of delivery to specific localities, and the scope of information that could be shared was not vast but rather limited only to what could be scrawled on a small piece of paper.

Time moved on, and the development of the printing press allowed for mass production of books and pamphlets. However, they were still limited in how they were transmitted. Next came radio and television, which greatly accelerated the ability to transmit information to a vast audience; but the information only flowed one way. The fax machine used phone lines to speedily send the written word but remained constrained because it did not allow for back-and-forth dialogue.

As you can see, even though information became more accessible, there was always some kind of barrier to accessing more of it. It was, and always has been, a give and take. There was no perfect solution. But now, with the Internet and the development of wireless networks and mobile devices, the transmission of words and video happen almost instantaneously from anywhere across the globe. Knowledge or data is available to almost anyone, at anytime, anywhere, and with no limitations outside of an individual's imagination or ability to access a data connection port or wireless router.

Like anything of value, the fundamentals of economics tell us that when the supply of a commodity is high, its value can be significantly reduced. Like all commodities, information is sensitive to the laws of supply and demand. With this great abundance of information, it's safe to say that it is just not as valuable as it used to be. To further illustrate, think about the value of a library. At one time, a freestanding library filled with books and computer access was undeniably important. You could find any book, any piece of information, and any type of data there. Now, libraries are next to obsolete. Information is vast. Only those who covet a hard copy of a book find meaning in a large building filled with books. The rest of us kick back with our smartphone, computer, or tablet to quench our thirst for information.

This is a significant departure from historical precedent when it was thought that information or knowledge was power. For thousands of years, knowledge was power for a whole host of reasons.

- *Information was parsed out in small bits. The vehicles for communication usually required some form of transmission that took time.*

- *Information was exclusive. Because it was a challenge to access, information was often guarded and protected.*

- *Information was expensive. The cost of information was high due to limited storage capabilities and high transmission costs.*

The game has changed. These have been all but eliminated with the capacity of chip technology and the speed of the Internet. Now, we can access information every second of the day on our mobile devices. Want to know who King Henry III was? Jump on the Internet. Need a recipe for beef Wellington? It's only a Siri or Google request away. Want to see how to fix the rollers on the garage door? You'll find many videos to choose from on YouTube.

An Age in Transition

We have rapidly transitioned away from the age of information, to the process age, the assimilation age, the human limitation age, or the application age - whichever phrase resonates with you. This has resulted from the significant gap between quantity and access to information and our ability as humans to process, manage, and act on the information to our benefit. We can only do so much with the data we digest. Knowledge is no longer the basis of power. It's not what you know; it's what you do with what you know that gets results.

Although the transition of accessing information has been dramatic, our ability as humans to process all the data is becoming increasingly stressed. Here's the lesson for leaders: we can transfer the idea of how to do something faster and more effectively, but that doesn't mean we can transition easily to doing it. The speed with which we can translate wisdom into action has not dramatically changed because our fundamental makeup as humans has not been drastically altered. Information comes at us faster, but our ability to utilize that same information remains constant.

We equate the speed of information transfer with a belief that actions and behaviors should be as transferable. We buy the idea that data and information have value, and we seek to accumulate as much of it as possible. It is like a large amount of wealth that we can never spend, nor can we take it with us to the grave. But history, precedent, and experience tell us information is truly valuable when it improves our insight and motivates each of us to act. *The value is in the insight or action, not the knowledge in and of itself.* Thought without action is meaningless, right? But we can only process so much of it to gain insight, and a smaller amount of that ever translates into real live action. In reality, the flow between data and insight gets backed up, and subsequently an even greater backup between insight and action occurs. What starts as a flowing faucet of information is eventually backed up by the challenge to develop insight and act.

We wonder:

- *What data do I use?*

- *What is accurate?*

- *What is the correlation to what I already know?*

- *What's the relationship between two points of view?*

- *Is it the truth or Internet legend?*

- *Can I rely on the source?*

All of these questions limit our ability as leaders to take data and use it to gain insight. And it doesn't stop there. Even if we get a glimmer of insight, we begin to consider questions like:

- *I have an idea of what to do, but can I do it?*

- *If I can, do I want to?*

- *Am I disciplined enough to change?*

- *What happens if I fail?*

- *How hard will doing this be?*

- *Am I committed to the outcome?*

- *Will it really work?*

So, then what happens? We create a lot of pressure. The backup of the flow of information from data to action begins to weigh on us. The water pressure that's built up in a clogged sink, pipe, or sewer can be significant, sometimes with the force equal to about ten times the air pressure of the tires on your car. Think of the weight of that amount of pressure. Physically, when individuals are carrying around a greater weight, they move more slowly, get tired quicker, and inevitably feel a greater burden.

Many people are walking around with the weight and pressure of abundant information on their backs. Access to the vast amount of information available today can feel like carrying the world on your shoulders. One result: Many people feel stressed in their work and careers. Their workload doesn't always cause the stress; many times, it's the overwhelming task of finding the right information, making sense of it, and the feeling that they should or could be doing more with it. It is like a quick trip to the buffet: You can load up on un-limited options, but then you overeat and regret you went in the first place.

According to a 2012 IBM survey of more than seventeen hundred CEOs in sixty-four countries, organizations feel the challenges that exist in this so-called information age. The abundance of detailed statistics, metrics, and big data analytics has created a glut of infor-mation and is a major obstacle for individuals and organizations. In the survey, the CEOs indicated that working in a data rich/insight poor company is one of their biggest obstacles. Leaders can be over-whelmed with accessing, filtering, and assimilating information and therefore have less of a capability to process and truly understand the meaning behind it. Just think of the hours lost during this process.

In organizations, senior management typically believes information automatically converts into action. Management implements new procedures because they are streamlined. They think that people will pick up on them automatically based on their talents. They suggest a new way to answer the phone in a call center and expect everyone will adopt the new process overnight. They offer people a one-day seminar on delegation, and as a result expect that supervisors will better manage their activities and workload immediately. It just doesn't work that way. Instead, translating information to action requires not only awareness but also incremental steps with repetition to ensure that some action happens.

Intuitively we know that information doesn't automatically translate to action or change. A beginning violinist can read volumes on the history of the instrument and techniques to perfect their craft. But information alone won't get them to Carnegie Hall. You can read every business book on organizational leadership there is, and even remember it all, yet still not become a better leader. There's more to it than just information and knowledge. So, with that said, let's shift away from the problem and move toward the solution.

Processing the Information Age

When any system processes more than it can manage, it becomes overloaded and tends to break down. That is just simple physics. A body inundated with alcohol for many years will have a significantly decreased liver function. When an accident occurs on the side of the road, the inevitable rubbernecking causes slowdowns on the highway and may lead to more accidents. A flower shop down a delivery driver on Valentine's Day will likely find many angry and frustrated customers and an overabundance of refunds, which will threaten the shop's cash flow and potentially its existence.

The glut of information can create the same effect, leading to suffering and overload. Endless research indicates that this information excess causes tremendous stress, significant distraction, and loss of productivity. The current human capacity to process loads of information is breaking down, and the technology and speed of information output has begun to exceed our ability to manage it. [6]

Pay Attention

But rest easy, as there is certainly hope. The opposite of information overload is the concept of attention management. Attention management flips the scenario to concentrate on the steps that can be taken to manage an abundance of information. Implementing attention management requires focus and the ability to understand the power and effectiveness of incremental improvement. It all starts with clarity and a commitment to what you need to know. That is, asking yourself what information you should seek or allow to enter your awareness. Attention management requires you to filter out the noise of information overload and focus on the things that are most important to you. Pablo Picasso said, "Art is the elimination of the unnecessary." These days, staying focused is an art.

The notion of attention management in organizations is a significant one.

- *The lack of attention management creates problems in effectiveness and significant stress. For example, information overload creates an irrational belief that the amount of work is also on overload. In working with thousands of people in the area of personal productivity, we continuously see that the number of tasks they need to complete need not be so overwhelming. The time spent distracted and unfocused is overwhelming, and it creates a feeling of poor production and little sense of accomplishment.*

---

[6] Zeldes, Nathan, David Sward, and Sigal Louchheim. "Infomania: Why we can't afford to ignore it any longer." First Monday. Accessed May 01, 2017. http://firstmonday.org/ojs/index.php/fm/article/view/1973/1848.

- *Supervisors work hard to manage the output of their employees, yet many of today's workforce operates away from their bosses or their teams, so it is no longer effective to monitor their workflow and observe their actions every minute. And the blending of work and personal information can no longer be balanced between "work time" and "personal time," as these two parts of our life are so deeply intertwined. The manager must really focus on keeping the attention of their employee. The manager can only hope to provide enough purpose, direction, support, and feedback to win the war for the employee's attention. Effective integration, not simply work/life balance, is the key to personal productivity, and leaders play a key role in their people's ability to pay attention.*

The good news: attention management can be learned. We don't have to be victims of information overload if we establish a personalized process that works for us. You might have heard the phrase "a war of attrition." It is defined as a struggle in which you harm your opponent in a lot of small ways so that they become gradually weaker. In other words, death by a thousand paper cuts.

In the processing age, a "war of attention" is being waged. It's fought in the battlefield inside the head of each employee, and the enemies are numerous. Social media, endless Internet distractions, poor instructions, lack of clarity on goals, and an overall dissatisfaction with work are all incrementally winning the battle. Author James Redfield said, "Where attention goes, energy flows."

Managers and leaders must be on the front lines of the attention management fight, battling for every hour and even minute of their employee's attention. Decreased productivity occurs when an employee's attention wanders to surfing the Web, checking on social media, or doing anything unrelated to work. Providing the proper reasons to earn and maintain employee attention is a key building block to elevating energy and the oft-evaluated employee engagement. Providing something as small as a clear set of instructions to something as large as a compelling organizational vision can accomplish this.

The implications of information overload can literally become a matter of life and death. Researchers are constantly studying the impact of health information technologies on health care. According to the *New York Times*, a recent study of a New York hospital indicated that electronic monitors produced more than 2.5 million alerts per month. But the sound emitted by a machine that indicates all is well and a machine that demands immediate attention is surprisingly similar. This creates a great deal of confusion in effectively recognizing life-threatening emergencies from false alarms, and it was a huge source of stress and burnout in the affected work group. [7]

So, what does this mean for us? Leaders should realize the process of using information is as important, or may be even more important, than the information itself. We might have all kinds of benchmarks and dashboards, but are they helping us make decisions and to act upon them?

Workers need to apply processing systems to understand and make sense of the information overload. The best leaders and managers think about this processing as a system itself, which they then must focus in the right direction. Good managers and leaders don't approach the gathering of information on a whim. They realize the processing of information is a core competency and have set ways of accumulating, analyzing, and evaluating all forms of information. They then apply the ideas that move the organization forward.

Taking Action

Beyond the gathering of information is the struggle to realize what to do with it. Effective leaders understand that the implementation

---

[7] Wachter, Robert M. "Why Health Care is Still So Bad." New York Times, March 21, 2015.

plan is as important, if not even more important, than the idea. In their book *The Knowing-Doing Gap*, Jeffrey Pfeffer and Robert Sutton give dozens of examples of organizations that invest in consultants whose advice is never acted on. Many times, the missing piece isn't present in knowing what to do, *it's found in doing it*. If we focus on progress instead of perfection, we can eliminate that cycle and start acting incrementally. After all, a B+ in practice is better than an A on the shelf. And a B+ organization working to improve over time is better than a blueprint for an A organization or idea that never happens because it is trying to be an A+ before action is ever taken.

One key approach to all of this: Leaders must realize they need to help employees process new information and change. They should attempt to give themselves time to translate data to insight and insight to action. They need to build that time into new initiatives, overall objectives, strategic plans, and tactical activities. Employees can only go as fast as their ability to process, and regularly exercising their processing muscles can improve that skill.

Three steps comprise the process from data to action:

1. *Filtering - Right Information.* Either personally or organizationally, systems should be developed to shrink the amount of information that is scanned to get what is needed. Like using a gatekeeper to reduce access, individuals should work to protect themselves from the noise of inappropriate and unnecessary information. This is the skill and process of clarifying what's truly most important. It takes time and multiple iterations because what's valuable today may not be valuable tomorrow.

2. *Processing - Gaining Insight.* Everyone certainly moves at his or her own speed. Leaders should work to understand that this isn't a measure of intelligence. For example, let's look at two people. In this case, we're going to represent intelligence as a

container that can hold one gallon of liquid. Each person has the same amount of intelligence, so they have containers that can each hold one gallon. However, one person has a bucket, and the other has a bottle. The bucket can absorb liquid much faster than the bottle, because its mouth is much wider. On the other side of the fence, liquid must be poured into the bottle much more carefully than the bucket. Information given to the individual with the bucket will be processed faster. The leader dealing with the individual who processes information through a bottleneck must give the new information slowly and deliberately. In reality, teams are made up of people with buckets and bottles, so the leader must be aware of that dynamic when it comes to processing data to gain insight. And just like pouring liquid, it can't be forced; it can only go as fast as the receiver can process it.

3. *Utilizing - Taking Proper Action.* Insight is no guarantee of action. All kinds of barriers can come into play when it comes to translating insight to action. These often include:

- *Is it the right action for the time and circumstance?*

- *Is the action aligned with objectives?*

- *Is it something that requires support?*

- *Does it need to be practiced before ingrained, and ingrained before mastered?*

For incremental improvement to occur, a crucial piece in this sequence needs to be considered. I often refer to this as the insight-action loop. Incremental improvement doesn't end when action is finally taken. As a matter of fact, it is not an ending, but more like the beginning of performance improvement. Some insight is gained only after action is taken. That action and its outcome can then inform greater insight, after which the process repeats itself. This is why acting on information is so important. An insight creates a desire for an action to be taken, the results of which impact the original insight, hone it, reinforce it, and then make it stronger or more focused. Incremental progress can come from this constant loop - the insight impacting the action, impacting the insight impacting the action. True progress comes when we allow, and are aware of, the impact of our new insight and the outcomes of the actions on each other. Let's look an illustration of this loop.

Some data - In the mid-1980s, data showed that Coke was losing market share to Pepsi. The loss had occurred slowly but surely over the previous fifteen years. [8]

Data to insight - Something needed to be done to reverse the slide. In reaction to this insight, the Coca-Cola Company created a new formula and tested it with over two hundred thousand consumers. It was proven to be a preferred taste.

Action taken - The company decided that to compete, Coke had to update its ninety-nine-year-old formula. On April 23, 1985, New Coke was introduced to the public.

Well, it didn't go according to plan. People rejected the new formula and responded negatively in unprecedented ways. By mid-June, the Coca-Cola Company was receiving almost fifteen hundred calls per day, compared to just four hundred before it changed the formula. This action was correctly seen as one of the biggest marketing blunders of all time, and at least one consumer hailed the CEO as "Chief Dodo."

---

[8]"The Real Story of New Coke." The Coca-Cola Company. November 14, 2012. Accessed May 01, 2017. http://www.coca-colacompany.com/stories/coke-lore-new-coke.

More data - However, the story doesn't end there. Because of that action, people remembered the drink they had taken for granted. They didn't want the drink they'd grown up with to change. The Coca-Cola Company realized that the people wanted the old formula back.

New insight - The insight the company gained from their ill-fated action was that Coca-Cola was not just a drink but rather a brand and a way of life for millions of people. The new insight led them to reinvigorate Coca-Cola Classic and brand sales soared. A classic case (pun intended) of the insight-action loop.

Information to Inches

To achieve incremental growth and performance improvement, you must understand the impact of the insight-action loop. Effective leaders seem to simplify the process of moving data to effective action. One key to incremental effectiveness: Don't do ten thousand things well, but do ten things well a thousand times.

My father was a genius at breaking things down into their key components. Whether he was studying a workflow process or working on a backyard patio, he would engage deeply in the details of that work. He always used to say that it wasn't a good thing to "be a jack of all trades, master of none." Effective leaders boil it all down to simple things that can be executed over and over. Let's look at some examples.

Famed football coach Vince Lombardi focused on a play called the sweep, as described in his book *Run to Daylight*. To work, the sweep leverages only a few key elements. Lombardi had his team practice it over and over and over until they had it down pat. The key was not in a bunch of complicated moves, but rather, in the effectiveness of execution. Even when the other team knew it was coming, the execution made the difference and the sweep was successful.[9]

When Jack Welch first took over GE in 1980, the company had more than forty-five business units and total revenues of $25.5 billion. In 1981, Welch announced they would leave any business line where they couldn't be the leader or a very close second. This led to an outcry from the public and some dismal predictions for the company's future. However, by the year 2000, the company grew to almost $130 billion in revenue, its stock outperformed the S&P 500 by more than three times its average return, and a forty-fold increase in stock price occurred, all with a reduction in business units to twelve in total.[10] The execution of Welch's decision made GE the empire that it is today.

There were many options available when Sergei Brin and Larry Page started Google. They recognized lots of possibilities to reach their goals. According to Brin, "When we set out in kind of the early Web days, we didn't decide to do online horoscopes or invitation services, but search, which is about information, which can make a real difference in people's lives." This degree of focus greatly impacted the direction of the company at the outset, and continues to inform how they do business today.

When Alan Mullaly joined Ford, the company had eighty-five different vehicle nameplates. He determined that it was very challenging to effectively execute all of the models. The company had the challenge of supporting numerous brands, all the associated supply challenges, all the dealer network complications, and many more moving pieces. The company made a decision, very unpopular at the time, to reduce

---

[9] Lombardi, Vince, W.C. Heinz, David Maraniss, John Madden, and Dave Anderson. Run to daylight!: Vince Lombardi with W.C. Heinz; new foreword by David Maraniss; introduction by John Madden and Dave Anderson. New York, NY: Simon & Schuster, 2014.

[10] Slater, Robert. *Jack Welch and the GE way: management insights and leadership secrets of the legendary CEO.* New York: McGraw-Hill, 2001.

the number of models they offered customers from eighty-five nameplates to twenty-two. The result: they increased their focus on quality and effectiveness while still being able to appeal to more than 90 percent of their prospective customers. Their incremental simplification led to excellent results. After surviving the recession and finding themselves as the only major automaker that didn't take a government loan, Ford realized enough profit in 2014 to pay every hourly worker an $8,800 bonus.

The previous examples are not complicated models or newly found solutions. The methods of simplifying information overload and focusing on the right things are all core principles that can be applied in any era and to any generation. We live in an age of abundant information that leads to increasing amounts of content. But steady analysis will not improve performance if we don't have a process for incremental development and allow for the insight-action loop.

When we apply this process, we can make changes that have a significant positive impact. The first step is admitting that this issue has a significant impact on all of us. If you are alive and breathing, you are likely afflicted by the same issues the rest of us face: too much knowledge, not enough application. The next steps in solving these issues are evaluating how to handle information overload, working to improve filtration, and implementing a program internally and externally for those you lead to manage their attention. This problem plagues us all, so let's work together to build strong systems, methods, and habits to better manage this flood of information.

Adept in Action:

- Are you frequently overwhelmed with all the information at your disposal? **Try this:** Eliminate all sources of new information (newspaper, TV, Twitter, Facebook) for three days and see what you miss.

- Does information overload slow you down and create analysis paralysis? **Try this:** Break down decisions into pro and con lists, where you can prioritize what's most important to you. Then run your ideas by action-oriented people and ask them what they would do.

- Do you feel unfocused, unable to stick to one path, and often confused about where to start when you're thrown off track? **Try this:** Make a prioritized list, separating what *must* be done from what *could* be done. Close out each day by reviewing the list to see what you accomplished and move the unfinished tasks forward.

- Do you ever look at how you absorb information and your ability to filter out what matters the most to you? **Try this:** Make a list of those five to six areas of your life that are most important to you at work and at home, and make sure you take action in those areas first before doing anything else.

- Do you want more tips and tools? **Try this:** Bookmark our website www.adeptleadership.com/tools-and-tips-adept-booksite/ to access a growing repository of valuable resources.

Chapter 3 – Attitude

The Significance of Habit of Thought

In 1929, people considered Winston Churchill neither a positive force nor a successful one. In fact, his conservative party in Britain was voted out of office. At the time, many considered him a right-wing extremist and believed he was completely out of touch with the people. He certainly had his own opinions and ideas, some of which he strongly held. Many examples of his strong will and independent nature throughout the years exist. History shows he performed poorly in his first formal schooling. It also paints him as a rebellious student and not the brightest color in the crayon box - it took him three attempts to pass the British Royal Military College exam. During the Boer War in South Africa, he worked as a war correspondent and was eventually taken as a wartime prisoner. Somehow, he managed to escape and traveled three hundred miles to safety in Mozambique. [11]

After Churchill joined the British government, he was unafraid to try and solve societal issues with unique and sometimes controversial legislation. When Britain found itself isolated and vulnerable to the growing Nazi regime, this accumulation of personal beliefs and tendencies served Churchill well. Shortly after being named prime minister, his words of determination, grit, and defiance (which represented

[11]"Winston Churchill." Biography.com. April 28, 2017. Accessed May 01, 2017. http://www.biography.com/people/winston-churchill-9248164.

his personal, deeply seated attitude of independence and courage) inspired a nation and helped build the coalition that would eventually go on to defeat the Nazi regime.

George W. Bush's behavior and words spoke loudly when he visited the rubble where the World Trade Center once stood. It was September 14, 2001, just three days after the collapse of the buildings. They still smoldered. First, he invited one of the firefighters, Bob Beckwith, to stand close to him to demonstrate to the world that America was standing together through that dark time. When someone in the crowd shouted out that they couldn't hear him, Bush adlibbed quickly, saying, "I can hear you – the rest of the world hears you – and the people who knocked these buildings down will hear all of us soon!"[12] Bush's behavior represented his attitude of strong will, action, determination, and an undeniable love of his country that resonated with the people there and throughout the world. Although later criticized for using those exact behaviors to make crucial decisions, at that moment, in that time, he delivered a powerful and unscripted message to the nation and the world that was clearly grounded in his personal convictions.

Actions from Choices

When we think of improving our personal performance and the performance of our own work groups, we often jump right into techniques and tactics we believe will be successful. We tend to apply concepts or actions that might work somewhere and at some time, without addressing the underlying causes of the current state. And in any specific form, the underlying causes of the results are usually the accumulation of actions people have taken.

---

[12] History.com. Accessed May 01, 2017. http://www.history.com/topics/reaction-to-9-11/speeches.

For example, your current financial position is usually an accumulation of all the actions you've taken to this point, unless you've inherited wealth or are one of the few who won the lottery. Those actions come from the choices you've made over time. Did you save early and often? Did you buy that stock on an unsubstantiated tip? Did you blow it all on red at the roulette wheel in Las Vegas? When we reach any result, it's because of the actions we've taken based on the choices we've made.

Just like Churchill and Bush, moments are often defined by a collection of experiences and decisions that shaped each of us well before we find ourselves in that particular moment. And sometimes it all comes together in perfect harmony.

That thinking may lead us to consider questions like:

- *What leads us to make our choices?*

- *Is someone forcing you to make certain choices?*

Habit of Thought

Sometimes our decisions result from external and uncontrollable forces, especially when we're young and our parents are trying to develop us and provide us with guardrails to stay on track. However, as we grow to adulthood, our choices become more and more our own. We are free to make choices and take the related actions to realize the outcomes that result from those actions. Usually, our choices are based on factors like our personality, upbringing, experiences, others' influence, and plenty of other external and internal factors that shaped us over time. But even so, one of the most important ingredients related to making choices and obtaining results is our attitude, defined as a predetermined way of thinking or feeling.

Paul J. Meyer had an impact on thousands of people through companies like Success Motivation Institute and Leadership Management, Inc. Some believe he is the father of the self-help movement and his ideas have had a big influence on me throughout my career. I have always especially appreciated his definition of attitude as a "habit of thought."

Like many habits, a habit of thought is ingrained and almost automatic. It kicks in when it's needed to produce the appropriate response. But here's the challenge: Some attitudes are contrary to the objectives people want to obtain.

Let's consider the lottery. Some people play it with the attitude that their problems will disappear if they only had more money. Then they win, and they have the attitude that they have more money than they ever hoped for so they might as well spend it on themselves, invest it with their friends who have great business ideas, and make sure they buy houses and cars for their loved ones.

However, it's said that most winners who were struggling financially before they won the lottery burn through most of their winnings within years of cashing the check. The flawed thinking that adversely affected their income is the same thinking that causes them to end up struggling again. The "money will solve my problems" attitude inevitably leads to poor spending choices and to the almost predestined outcome of having no money at all. Conversely, many wealthy individuals can point to times when they weren't as wealthy and had lost a great deal but maintained the habitual behaviors to make the right choices and corrective actions to rebuild their wealth.

Here's an example of how a habit of thought can limit success in the workplace: what if I asked you to complete the following sentence, "If you want something done right . . ."

What came to mind? Did you quickly come up with an answer?

The common response is, "Then you have to do it yourself!"

This response is so automatic, it's likely deeply ingrained in your mind. Now, if you are one of the many managers with that attitude, you may be resistant to accepting ideas or techniques relative to accomplishing tasks through your team or your colleagues. Simply put, you feel like you are at it alone. But no one person is an island. You may resist delegation because things always come back to you worse off than when they left. You assign responsibility, but in the end, you have to do it anyway. You reject dedicating time to training because it takes twice as long for you to teach others than if you just did something without their help. In reality, you can become well versed about the topic of delegation, but you'll never make any substantial progress unless you understand that your attitude is at cross-purposes and counter-productive.

This shows that information isn't the only key to learning and performance improvement. Many organizations invest in learning libraries and corporate universities with lots of content. But here's the challenge: They have no focus on calibrating exactly how a person perceives an issue before they are exposed to that content. Individuals who might benefit the most from the content may not be aware of their need to improve in that area or are not aware of their limiting habits. So, they take the classes, but nothing changes, even if they learn the information. This occurs in most formal training in the workplace. When organizations incorrectly focus on content and information transfer as the key component of training, they quickly become disillusioned with formal training. That's because it doesn't produce the performance changes they're looking for.

At the individual level, meaningful change occurs when an attitude shifts or when an individual is held accountable to act in a certain way long enough so that the outcomes of the new actions influence their thinking and establish a new habit of thought. Essentially, they replace limiting thoughts with productive action. Either way, the only sustainable change occurs when an attitude has changed.

Ask any ex-smoker about the challenges of quitting. The majority will say they were only successful when their attitude about smoking changed. Sometimes that occurs through a traumatic experience, resulting in a sudden and abrupt shift in attitude. However, most often they quit smoking by taking action through a program of denial or benefit that eventually produces outcomes that impacted their previous attitude.

A key element of incremental change is that it allows you to develop an awareness of when deeply ingrained attitudes are preventing progress. As a leader, realize your team is comprised of an accumulation of ingrained attitudes, created well before you met any of your employees. It's then critically important to consider that actions come from choices that are made and choices come from attitudes. To sustain change, aim for impacting the attitudes of those experiencing change. Like any other habit, attitude usually needs the passage of time to be truly affected. Attitudes incrementally progress.

Think about a professional golfer looking to gain an advantage. They may be at the top of their game but continue to look at how they can change their grip, stance, how they shift their bodyweight, the position of the ball, and their follow through. And so on and so forth. Immediately, they may see a decrease in their performance because the old swing was so ingrained, but eventually they hope to improve their results. When a swing is so habitual, it takes not just time but also small changes to the mechanics to produce the desired outcome. The same is true when shifting any habit, especially those ingrained in your mind. It not only takes time; it takes practice and repetition doing it the right way; it is truly a game of inches.

We're already aware that the laws of incremental improvement can impact attitudes, just like other habits. But information overload can also affect attitudes, which we mentioned earlier, and can restrict and pinch the growth of positive attitudes, which is why attention management is so important. Without such focus, people become confused about what to do and how to do it. They waste lots of time and energy and become ineffective and constantly stressed. After all, garbage in, garbage out. Information overload can negatively impact personal attitudes.

Organizational Attitude

How do attitudes impact organizations? Leaders' habits of thought can significantly affect those around them. Although organizations certainly can't limit the information people absorb or relate to, they can influence it through what they choose to focus on.

Take Chick-fil-A. Every Sunday, the company closes the doors of all its locations so that associates can spend time with friends and family. The founder's Christian beliefs clearly inform this practice. Some people support Chick-fil-A simply because of this Christian foundation. Others support it because of its delicious chicken sandwiches. Of course, others go out of their way to avoid the restaurant chain simply because they do not share the same belief system as the founding family. So even though the organization doesn't mandate certain beliefs, focusing on those habits of thought has a huge impact. In organizations, culture is simply an accumulation of the attitudes of their employees. Attitudes not only significantly impact the actions and outcomes of individuals, but the collective actions and outcomes of organizations overall.

Creating Better Habits

Armed with the knowledge that habits are ingrained and created over time, how can we best shift the paradigm and motivate people to change negative or limiting habits to positive ones? Leadership within an organization may consider attitude a predetermined and uncontrolled soft skill set that comes with the employee. But attitudes aren't soft and fuzzy things. They are the catalyst for all performance improvement. They are the engine of organizational engagement. One outcome of effective leadership is the influence these leaders can have on the attitudes of individuals.

If you look at attitude as a habit of thought and consider that habits can be developed, you'll better understand the impact of leadership on attitude. After all, leaders have a considerable influence on the habits of their people in more tangible ways. For example, if the leader tends to dress more casually, then the team adopts a more casual approach. If the leader uses more colorful language, those that tend to use that language feel more comfortable in doing so. The same is true of attitude and its potential to be adopted by those people in direct contact with the leader.

Employees and teams often become more resilient, positive, tenacious, or vulnerable if they see those traits in upper management. In terms of management, one of the most impactful subsections under the umbrella of positive attitude is the practice of gratitude. Gratitude is a combination of the words "great" and "attitude." Think about it. Have you ever seen someone who was truly grateful not have a positive impact on others? Of course not. A leader should never underestimate the impact of his or her habits of thought on others. Just as children watch and observe their parents and often mimic their behaviors, employees watch their leaders like a hawk, picking up on small and large characteristics alike.

The insight-action loop, which we discussed in Chapter 2, significantly impacts the development of attitude. Typically, performance improvements come easier if attitude changes lead the way. For example, consider the above-referenced conversation regarding the notions of "*if you want something done right, do it yourself*" versus "*if you want something done right, invest the time to train people in the right way.*" If you shift your own attitude and begin saying the latter to everyone, you will find it easier to adopt it as a belief, and your actions will change as well. However, sometimes, to improve performance, you may establish a behavior or action even when you don't really believe it or "feel it." You may try a new tactic even if you're not firmly committed to the idea. But if you begin to see beneficial change, you'll adopt the behavior because you value the result.

Sometimes the action informs the insight in the insight-action loop. When it comes to attitude, actions or behaviors over time can have an impact on improving attitude. Practicing an action long enough and recognizing positive results can help you change your mind about previous thoughts. So, if I force myself to invest some time in training and developing my people, soon the outcomes they produce will help me realize they CAN do the job and I don't have to do it all myself.

I had an employee who was a great performer. She hit all her goals and was always among our best people. After she had children, she recognized that her performance had slightly diminished. After some self-evaluation, she also recognized that a tough start to the day with her children impacted how she dealt with clients. The harder the start, the more difficult the workday. To change this, she focused on turning up the volume of positivity on her first couple of calls. She was the kind of person whose smile lit up the room, so she focused on slapping on that smile during those difficult mornings, even when she didn't feel like it. This led to magnificent results. Her clients favorably responded and even commented on how her upbeat and positive attitude brightened their day. She found that faking it until she made it invited positive feedback from her customers and naturally lifted her attitude too.

This is where guidance, accountability, and feedback come in. If an employee is required to perform certain tasks, is held accountable to that performance, and then receives feedback, they may also begin to achieve new and unexpected outcomes. Those results can change their mindset about any issue. Only when they change their mind or attitude will the change be sustainable because the thought has become their own.

I worked with a woman who was an individual contributor. Although she was viewed as a "Hi-Po," someone having high potential, she insisted that she "would never, EVER, want to be a manager." I accepted that decision, yet had her start doing some additional management tasks. I held her accountable to complete those tasks, offered discussions, and provided feedback about the outcomes. Over the course of a few weeks, she valued the results she achieved and became aware that those tasks were a part of the managerial role. Soon, she realized that she enjoyed those results and the tasks . . . and that her previous mindset and habit of thought about management had been totally inaccurate. Suddenly, she became excited about moving into management. She told me, "I had no idea what being a manager was about, and I changed my mind." The outcome of her actions had informed and impacted her attitude. She became a great manager.

Actions that don't work or produce poor results can negatively affect attitudes too. It's often said that insanity is doing things over and over the same way but expecting different results. Sometimes when results aren't produced, you establish the attitude that it'll never work for you, and you begin trying anything to solve the problem.

As an avid former baseball player, we refer to this as the "slump mentality." Sometimes we find ourselves so frustrated with outcomes that we start changing unrelated things to see if we can change the results. In baseball, this can lead to superstitious behavior because we can't figure out what else is going wrong. Players get a hit and realize they were wearing their wristbands inside out, or sitting at the end of the bench, so they repeat *that* behavior, hoping to get the same results.

Where you sit and what you wear, however, has nothing to with how you hit the ball. You might even know colleagues who practice this behavior. They show up to work every day with mismatched socks because they got the big deal and broke the slump when they wore their mismatched plaid socks.

Unfortunately, this behavior becomes part of the problem. It gets us away from practicing the principles that we know work, and this can elongate the "slump." But we should always return to the basics. Fundamentals have a multiplier effect on results. When they are off, or out of sync, it becomes a huge challenge to produce results. We make unnecessary modifications to processes or we throw out systems that typically work, only because one step missed the mark. This is reactive and impatient behavior. A salesperson with a two-call method of connecting with new prospects runs into a dry spell. Instead of sticking with things and realizing they will turn around, he eliminates one of the calls and is frustrated when the results don't improve.

Leaders should never assume the fundamentals are intact. They need to be diligent about supporting and reinforcing the fundamentals to ensure that their people are achieving their full potential. You must not fall into the trap of assuming that an experienced employee must be a person who practices the basics. I can't tell you how many leaders we've worked with who have been managing for years but didn't practice or even know the fundamentals of managing others.

A year before he was hired to coach the Green Bay Packers, Vince Lombardi was a little-known assistant for the New York Giants. At the time, the Packers were absolutely terrible. They had won exactly one game in the previous season and had lost more than seventy games in the 1950s. Players dreaded being traded to or drafted by the NFL's "Siberia." When Lombardi took over, he quickly focused on the fundamentals. He analyzed the talent on the team and got rid of players who didn't live up to his expectations, including the dominant player in the Packers locker room the year before. He instilled discipline and conditioning and repeated the same plays until he was satisfied the players had perfected them. Despite strong protests and a significant uproar, he stayed the course of his convictions and beliefs. After they won their first game of the season, the players were so surprised and excited by the result that they carried Vince off the field and gave him the game ball. Based on their reaction, you'd think they'd won the Super Bowl. [13]

Lombardi had required certain actions of his players. He held them accountable to those actions and provided guidance and feedback even when they didn't believe. Those outcomes led to achievements that finally changed their attitudes about what they could do and how they could do it. They began to regularly produce those outcomes because those attitudes had become their own. They won seven games in 1959. They played for the title in 1960 and won the Super Bowl in 1961. They began a reign that made Green Bay known as "Titletown" and Lombardi a legend.

In organizations today, leaders should ensure that new initiatives account for the potential resistance of attitudes. The organizational concept that people are more committed to things they participate in creating takes this into account. During an organization change initiative, involve those who are closest to the issue in the solution. Harvard business professor Rosabeth Moss Kantor says, "When change is done by us it's exhilarating, when it's done to us it's debilitating."

Involving employees in decision-making and large-scale change processes can have a huge impact on the results of the change initiative. People like to feel like they are a part of a purposeful and meaningful shift. Often, they resist it when they don't feel as if they are heard or involved. I'm not talking about decisions by consensus here. The leader or leaders still have the final say. The difference: There is a

---

[13] Maraniss, David. *When Pride Still Mattered: A Life of Vince Lombardi.* NY, NY: Simon & Schuster, 1999.

process for hearing the concerns of those involved, addressing those concerns, and then clarifying why the decision was made. Employees can understand when their idea has not been accepted or a decision goes contrary to their recommendation. They don't understand when a change that impacts their work is decided with no input from them at all.

In 1980, the Harley-Davidson Motor Company teetered on the brink of bankruptcy. The company turned around when a band of loyal insiders with a passion for the history of the company and a belief it could be saved took it over. They implemented the latest Japanese production system and made significant changes within the organization that were not accomplished by previous corporate initiatives. The company went from the brink of bankruptcy to become a Fortune 500 company known for lasting quality.[14]

One of the most important results of effective leadership on an organizational level is attitude impact. If we think of attitude as a habit of thought, it follows that culture is really the collective attitude of an organization. Culture runs deep and is the lifeblood of any organization; you might define culture as the collective actions and behaviors of an organization over time. Where do those actions come from? They originate from the choices the organization makes. We know choices come from habits of thought or attitudes, so it's safe to say that culture is organizational attitude. If you believe that individuals can influence others' attitudes, then leaders can and do have substantial impact on the culture of any organization.

The electoral map provides a classic example of how attitude can be influenced by those who are close to one another. Why do "red states" and "blue states" exist? They represent the cultural attitudes of an area. They also speak to how hard it is to change culture. Organizations must understand this dynamic. A change initiative can't easily

---

[14] Rifkin, Glenn. "How Harley Davidson Revs Its Brand." Strategy Business. October 01, 1997. Accessed May 01, 2017. https://www.strategy-business.com/article/12878?gko=ffaa3.

be rolled out unless it's in alignment with current culture or if it's given time to nurture and grow to help the culture incrementally change.

In summary, attitude has a huge impact on the performance of individuals and how they work as a team. If we consider attitudes as habits of thought, we can truly understand that like any habit, with the right actions, feedback, and support, these attitudes can be changed, developed, and improved incrementally.

Adept in Action:

- Our habit of thought impacts our choices and the actions we take to produce our results or outcomes. **Try this:** Become aware of how you think about new and different situations to see if you have any attitudes that are holding you back.

- You may discover that you have a habit of thought that is limiting your progress. **Try this:** Create actions you can do, and repeat these actions to begin seeing more positive results.

- You may feel stuck and can't seem to make progress. **Try this:** Make sure you're practicing the fundamentals effectively by seeking feedback from someone with an outside perspective.

- Involving people in any change initiative gains their full commitment and engagement. **Try this:** Get people involved in the change early in the process so you can respond to their suggestions and gain the benefit of their knowledge and experience.

- Do you want more tips and tools? **Try this:** Bookmark our website   www.adeptleadership.com/tools-and-tips-adept-booksite/ to access a growing repository of valuable resources.

Chapter 4 – Discipline

Making the Commitment to Achieve Success

The word *commitment* often conjures intense personal reactions. Some people break out in hot sweats when they hear the word, while others immediately begin to consider how much work the act of *committing* to something, to anything, will take. But if success is elusive (and it is), then it is through commitment that we catch it and make it our own. World Champion racecar driver Mario Andretti said, "Desire is the key to motivation, but it's determination and commitment to an unrelenting pursuit of your goal - a commitment to excellence - that will enable you to attain the success you seek." Each of us has the capacity to commit, to unequivocally decide to apply our energy, effort, and purpose to fulfilling a goal. Once we say, "I am in," we can begin to realize success.

The Definition of Discipline

In the previous chapters, we talked about the impact of an incremental approach, the importance of attention management, and the role and importance of attitude in creating performance improvement. However, all of this requires a stick-to-itiveness, and the desire to make sure those changes occur. If I tried to sell this concept to you and called it *discipline*, many of you would feel deflated. You may think,

"Here we go again. Someone is going to give me a formula for success that is going to be really constraining and force me to do things I don't even want to do." In reality, we are going to talk about the absolute need for discipline in making change and improving performance. This is just a must. There is no way around it. However, here's the good news: As you read these pages, you may just think about discipline in a whole new way - one that really works for you.

The word *discipline* has different definitions and carries different meanings to people across the board. For some, it means spanking or any form of corporal punishment. Others think of discipline as a necessary and negative evil. And at times the meaning of discipline is grounded in structure, systems, and regimentation. But to understand how discipline impacts performance improvement, we should look at it through a unique paradigm to better determine what it is and what it is not.

Consider the following example:

Jim wants to get in better shape, so he commits to going to the gym at five thirty every morning. Through sheer will and determination, he accomplishes this goal for a while, mostly because he's sick and tired of being out of shape. One morning he misses his workout because his alarm clock doesn't go off. He swears he will pick up his gym routine again and stay focused on doing it every day. However, the following day he misses his workout because he forgets to bring his gym clothes, but he wills himself to go the next couple of days after that. Soon, he misses another day and starts becoming frustrated that he's not disciplined enough to work out every day like he committed to do. After a while, with continued hits and misses, he focuses so much on the times he misses that he decides he can't keep up the pace and quits the regimen altogether.

Does that scenario and outcome sound familiar?

Jim's experience occurs to a lot of people who are trying to change. They start by thinking regimentation is the only path to achieve their objective. They feel that only a perfect regimen will help them get over the hump and finally reach their goal. As soon as they don't perfectly comply with their plan, they feel as though they are failing. Once they see they are falling short of perfect, they become frustrated and give up on the idea of making the change altogether. They say, "Discipline isn't for me."

The challenge here is the mindset regarding discipline. Regimentation is not the same as discipline. Regimentation is defined as being strictly organized or controlled. The key word here is *strictly*, with little room for deviation or variance. You can be disciplined to a goal, a principle, or objective without having to achieve it in a strictly controlled way. In fact, most goals allow for a little wiggle room. Effective discipline can allow for some flexibility in the "how" as long as you remain true to the "what."

We see this often in our work with so-called "creative types" or individuals with a more "flexible" personality. They absolutely resist tight control of anything that they perceive to be strict. To them, significant structure constrains, creates unnecessary tension, and may be an obstacle to freedom and creativity. Because they perceive regimentation as the suggested way to be disciplined, they believe that discipline is not for them. Here's the key: discipline is essential for performance improvement, but it can exist without regimentation.

Achieving discipline with regimentation is like creating music through an orchestra. However, achieving discipline without regimentation is like playing jazz music. According to the Thelonious Monk Institute of Jazz, "Individual musicians have the freedom to express themselves on their instrument as long as they maintain their responsibility to the other musicians by adhering to the overall framework and structure

of the tune." Each member has "individual freedom but with responsibility to the group."[15] Discipline without regimentation works the
same way. You have freedom in the way you go about achieving the
objective, but not in what you achieve. Some people like symphony
music and some people like jazz, but it's all good music. Pure regimentation can restrict improvisation. Sometimes, improvising can
raise the performance to a whole new level.

It's probably not the most productive thing to focus on regimentation
without regard to the outcome. It would be like someone with severe
OCD trying to accomplish a task before conducting certain rituals.
It may restrict their performance even if it means they are perfect in
their regimentation. Conversely, performers who have no regimentation will never be able to play in an orchestra or a jazz ensemble
because the "music" they make will be unrecognizable. Peak performance comes when there's an appropriate balance between discipline
and the regimentation necessary to help the individual reach the goal.

The key to discipline is to know which "style of music" works most
effectively for you and to understand that unregimented discipline
can be as impactful as strict regimentation.

The Shift to Positive Discipline

Discipline becomes positive when we focus less on what we must do
or give up and more on that to which we are committed. In response
to a question about his commitment to music, Luciano Pavarotti said,
"People think I'm disciplined. It's not discipline. It is devotion. There
is a great difference." The word *devotion* places the focus of discipline
in the mindset and attitude toward what you're moving toward. Devotion is defined as love, loyalty, or enthusiasm for a person, activity,

[15] "What is Jazz?" Jazz in America. Accessed May 01, 2017. http://www.jazzinamerica.org/
LessonPlan/5/1/242.

or cause, and that's what positive discipline truly is. Rather than being forced, it creates a space for commitment to occur and the resulting action to follow.

Sometimes, regimentation *can* help you become more disciplined. Committing to a certain way, staying structured in that way, and doing it over and over can help you see positive outcomes so your devotion to the change becomes sustainable. At work, you may get feedback that your subordinates don't feel recognized. You may not agree with the feedback and may not think it's worthwhile, but you commit to making the necessary effort to recognize employees because your boss has made that "suggestion." So, you begin planning a certain time each week to think about and then thank subordinates. After doing this for a while, you see that the employees seem to be doing more work and are getting things done at a faster rate. Your agreement to recognize employees has led to an appreciation for that outcome and a greater commitment to providing recognition. The simple act of doing it has increased your discipline.

Let's apply this same theory to your personal life. You begin getting up at a certain time each day to ensure that you go to the gym. Being successful at this incrementally, not perfectly, reinforces the value of exercise and you become more committed to it. Remember the insight-action loop. Sometimes the outcomes inform and reinforce the actions and they move in a positive direction. Regimentation can be beneficial for some, but it's the development of a greater commitment to the outcome that keeps it sustainable.

Discipline can be achieved without regimentation. It is easier to be committed when you become firmly focused on an end in mind and the objective is crystal clear. In the early years developing the personal computer, Steve Jobs was seen as being tirelessly driven toward the goal of a PC on everybody's desktop. He provided perspective on this observation later when he said, "If you are working on something exciting that you really care about you don't have to be pushed, the vision pulls you."[16] He was devoted or disciplined to it and working on it didn't feel like a tremendous effort. True discipline looks challenging to the observer, yet it can be effortless to the individual doing it because he or she is being pulled along by his or her commitment to the desired future state. To be disciplined means to be totally, absolutely committed to an outcome.

Organizations can prosper by applying corporate discipline and staying focused on their vision, purpose, and values. In 1982, a never-before-seen crisis occurred. Seven people were reported to have died in Chicago after taking extra strength Tylenol capsules. The product had been tampered with on store shelves. No one knew the extent of the issue. Johnson & Johnson faced significant losses from its number one product, especially if the company removed all the inventory from their Chicago stores. However, based on statements in their credo about protecting people first, they recalled every bottle in the entire country, even though they were not responsible for the tampering and their action could lead to devastating financial results.

After the company pulled the product, it worked on a solution to prevent tampering from happening again. Johnson & Johnson developed a new type of bottle. When Tylenol returned to the shelves, it gained popularity because it was guaranteed to be safe long before its competitors. This led to the development of the industrywide tamperproof bottles that we see today. The 1980s Tylenol incident has become a classic crisis management case. It illustrates how an organization stayed disciplined to its commitment, carrying out the activity without regard to consequence because they held the belief so strongly.[17]

---

[16] Meah, Asad. "20 Most Memorable Quotes From Steve Jobs." AwakenTheGreatnessWithin. February 21, 2016. Accessed May 1, 2017. http://awakenthegreatnesswithin.com/20-most-memorable-quotes-steve-jobs/.

[17] Markel, Dr. Howard. "How the Tylenol murders of 1982 changed the way we consume medication." PBS. Accessed May 01, 2017. http://www.pbs.org/newshour/updates/tylenol-murders-1982.

Discipline doesn't start in the doing. It starts with an attitude of discipline or the commitment to those things we really want. The failure of the diet doesn't start in the eating. It begins with the way we think about food and what we devote ourselves to. Thinking about food as comfort commits us to the short-term feelings of pleasure rather than the long-term dissatisfaction we'll have from being overweight or unhealthy. It is an impulsive and nearsighted approach.

Living and Loving the Gap

In implementing any kind of incremental improvement process, you are constantly aware of where you are in terms of your objectives. If you do it right, you'll know the difference between the goal and your current performance or outcomes. I've been told that some people find it debilitating to feel like they are always falling short. I've had many clients say they'd rather not know something because it's just too painful. However, it's often said that people who are successful "fail" a lot more than people who don't achieve what they want. The difference is in their perspective of "failures." People who don't achieve their objectives tend to label themselves as failures and get stuck when they refuse to act after a setback. They say, "Well, I'll never do that again." Or they decide that they were somehow inadequate or unable.

By contrast, successful people don't put the same label on "failure." They consider the setback as just another opportunity along the way. They love knowing where they stand, regardless whether a gap exists between actual performance and where they want to be. They have the mindset of constructive discontent, that they may be displeased with where they are, but they are not defeated in their mindset or dissuaded from their efforts.

In graduate school, my professor of strategy, Dr. Diana Wong, introduced us on the first day of class to the vast and varied workload we would be asked to complete. We were all aghast at the amount of homework she assigned. As working professionals, we knew that none of us could possibly finish all the work, maybe not even half of it. But Dr. Wong assured us she would not yield and that we would work through it. Amazingly, she communicated this overwhelming circumstance with a huge smile.

Dr. Wong knew her class was demanding and rigorous, but the pure joy she portrayed in guiding us through it inspired us. She wanted us to realize the iterative value of learning, to understand what it felt like to fall short but still enjoy the process, to appreciate pushing our boundaries, and to achieve more than we thought was humanly possible. Dr. Wong was the first teacher I ever had who made rigor fun and helped me learn to not only live with but enjoy knowing the difference between where I was and where I wanted to be.

Since then I've become increasingly aware of the impact your attitude has on the gap between where you are and where you want to be. If you focus your energy on failure, dissatisfaction, and harshly judge yourself on outcomes that fall short, you will struggle. If you seem to be aware of the gap and treat it as data, without judgement, you will more easily make progress. You've got to love the gap.

Corporate Discipline

In organizations, you must take a big picture perspective to clearly communicate what you are devoted to. This might be the mission or purpose of the organization or it's guiding principles. In this way, employees can decide if it's something they want to be a part of. They can stay committed to those principles in the face of obstacles and challenges, just like the dieter is committed to the outcome of losing weight when the challenges of eating other foods come into play.

The best leaders reinforce the devotion the organization should be committed to on a consistent basis. They do it for the big picture issues and some small issues that are important to them. Companies that have corporate discipline thrive. They are devoted to certain practices, beliefs, behaviors, and outcomes. Corporate discipline can be applied in many forms, including:

- *Starting and ending meetings on time*

- *Handling conflict appropriately*

- *Recognizing good performance*

- *Providing clear and consistent feedback*

- *Having consistent consequences for poor behavior*

- *Treating others with dignity and respect even through conflict*

- *Performance checks and balances*

Discipline is simply clarifying what you are devoted to and acting to reinforce that devotion on a consistent basis. To effectively apply it, there's another important ingredient: focus.

The Power of Focus

When we talked about information, we discussed the challenge of information overload. Resisting information overload requires filtering what information we allow through our safeguards, our attention management. It is easy to be devoted to all of our work tasks with the same energy and passion, but we struggle to accomplish them all effectively. Choices need to be made to differentiate between priorities to ensure the important stuff gets done, and done in the right way. This is where the concept of focus comes in. Focus is critical to discipline.

So, how does focus work?

Archimedes, a Greek mathematician and inventor, was said to be responsible for a technique that defended the city of Syracuse from the Romans in 215 BC. According to legend, he used a series of mirrors to redirect the light of the sun toward the oncoming ships. This created an intense light that sparked kindling on the decks, which burst into flames and engulfed the dry wooden ships in fire. Archimedes's invention didn't create any new energy; he just magnified its power and directed it in exactly the right way. Whether that story is a myth or part of history, Archimedes understood the power of focus. He also created the fulcrum, a leveraged pivot point for lifting objects. We consider focus to be a fulcrum for performance to leverage effort so that it magnifies and directs it in a way that has the most beneficial results.[18] We can apply Archimedes's principles to getting things done and being more productive.

Focus seems to come easily when there is no choice.

- *When a family emergency occurs, you forget the worries and pressures of day-to-day life that were overwhelming you and tend to the issues at hand.*

- *When you are extremely involved in your tasks at work and are truly immersed and enjoying them, time just flies by.*

[18] "Archimedes." Ancient Greece. Accessed May 01, 2017. http://www.ancientgreece.com/s/People/Archimedes/.

- *When a woman is in labor, she is no longer thinking about the furnishings of the baby's room or the thank you notes for the shower. It's time to breathe and PPUUSSHHH!*

Most of the time, it's not easy to stay focused because we face an abundance of choices. People experience focus as being "in the zone." For that to occur, real focus combines mindfulness and mindlessness in a unique way. Athletes understand and use the power of the fulcrum of focus to reach peak performance.

When Tiger Woods was on his amazing run of winning championships, he was asked about a particularly challenging putt he needed to make in the 2008 US Open. The sportscaster, Mike Greenberg, on the *Mike and Mike* radio program was wondering about all the thoughts going through Woods's head considering the amazing pressure he faced and enormity of that moment. If Woods made the putt, he would tie the leader. But if he missed, he would lose. Greenberg suggested these permutations that could occur and asked Woods how he could handle the implications of all those thoughts going through his mind. In response, Woods said that he was simply thinking "firm, left edge," meaning he was focused on nothing but how he would strike the ball and where he would aim it. That's it - no implications, worries, or distractions; just two simple things to focus on in a situation where he could have had a thousand things going through his mind.

Focus is the ultimate representation of the old expression, "How do you eat an elephant? One bite at a time." Focus requires breaking down an objective into bite-sized pieces so they can be the central thought toward your effort. Focus is contrary to the popular marketing notion that "you can have it all." Having it all is impossible and unrealistic. However, with proper focus you *can* achieve most of the things you really, really, really want.

Focus is also key to performance for organizations. On a macroscale, what an organization focuses on can be critical to their success or failure. Swiss time makers lost a great deal of market share to digital competitors when they shifted their focus to the mechanics of watchmaking, rather than LED components.

Kmart diluted their focus on retail by going after other business lines. As a result, they lost market share to Walmart. That competitor was focused on their internal operations, and by revolutionizing retail supply chain management, they left rival Kmart in the dust. [19]

Focus is also critical on the individual level in organizations. If people are all over the place, they just can't be effective. Leaders can help individuals focus by eliminating the "noise in the system" and help them navigate the information overload. If confusing messages are coming down from corporate, they can filter what's crucial and help their people stay on top of what's most meaningful to getting their job done. Leaders can help people prioritize around distractions and obstacles and remind them of what's truly most important.

Focus is a stepping stone to discipline. It sharpens it and is a catalyst for making it happen. To focus effectively, narrow the possibilities and distractions. This comes from keeping your eye on the target. Focus is not easy to come by. It doesn't just happen. It's a matter of critical thinking, strategic planning, and specific execution.

Building the Environment for Discipline

It's been said that success is doing what others aren't willing to do. One of the ironic facts about the secret of success in many endeavors is that there really are no secrets. The laws of incremental improvement help

---

[19] "Kmart Vs. Wal-Mart: A Study in Supply Chain Approaches." Apptricity Blog. Accessed May 01, 2017. https://blog.apptricity.com/2013/12/kmart-vs-wal-mart-a-study-in-supply-chain-approaches/.

you see the flow of moving toward a goal or objective and staying committed to that path over the long run.

Back in my pharmaceutical business days, I had many opportunities to recommend our products to new doctors. Many would switch the product they used based on the last representative with whom they met. At first, I thought those were the people I wanted to convince because I could get them to use my products immediately and make an impact. My manager helped me realize that the real target was the doctors who were very difficult to see and hard to convince. If I could get them on my side, it would be very hard for others to swoop in and steal the business. These actions wouldn't make my numbers look immediately impressive. However, if I could handle the short-term frustrations and slower sales and keep my efforts focused on the overall objective, I believed that I could exceed my goals for the territory.

When applied incrementally, this is kind of how discipline works. Instead of doing an on again, off again yo-yo diet, where it's either perfect or not at all, you need to stay focused on the long-term objective, which is losing weight. It helps you to clearly see the picture of what you want in the long run and focus on how you will feel when you get there, not just the results you see today.

In the 1960s, a Stanford researcher studied the power of delayed gratification. In his famous marshmallow test, Walter Mishel's researchers gave nursery school students the choice to eat a marshmallow right away or wait fifteen minutes to eat it and get an extra treat. Those nursery school students were then tracked over the following decades. The children who had been able to wait the fifteen minutes to get their treat ended up being much healthier, had better relationships, and enjoyed greater professional success.[20] A more recent study added to the previous one by indicating this outcome is somewhat situational and

---

[20] "40 Years of Stanford Research Found That People With This One Quality Are More Likely to Succeed." James Clear. February 10, 2017. Accessed May 01, 2017. http://jamesclear.com/delayed-gratification.

that trust was a huge factor in waiting for the delayed reward. Either way, here's the essential conclusion: The individual participant must be convinced they are delaying their satisfaction for something worth waiting for.

Focus convinces us that we have something worth waiting for. It helps us "believe it before we see it" and make that mindset a reality over time.

The ability to focus isn't a one and done process. It's easy to get distracted as we go through our day-to-day experience. Focus occurs as we execute along the way. For example, the idea of managing our time is really about managing energy to accomplish what we want most to do and what is essential to organizational results. To help people stay on track for accomplishing those things, we employ the idea of Primary Focus Areas, or PFAs.

PFAs are a set of tasks categorized together. They help employees stay on track for accomplishing what matters most to the organization. They help filter out all the other activities that can distract from achieving objectives. They are not specific objectives, but categories of activities that can help accomplish those objectives. A salesman might look at prospecting as a primary focus area in addition to activities to serve his or her existing clients. This PFA reminds the salesperson that although there might be plenty of business today, he or she needs to do some prospecting each day to keep the future pipeline alive.

For a supervisor, the PFAs may be based on coaching and training people. It's easy to slip back into doing the work him or herself, but with a PFA to help remember to conduct coaching activities, the supervisor can stay on track toward developing a team rather than doing the work him or herself. PFAs help workers remember and keep track of what they are really committed to achieve.

The Goals of Delayed Gratification

Experiments with delayed gratification also point out the value of setting goals. Goal setting is not a controversial topic as goals have been proven to work as a motivational tool. The key is to allow goal setting to incrementally work. This will often reveal:

- *Limitations in your ability. You may not have the skill to become a professional golfer, so you may need to modify the goal or at least the outcomes expected.*

- *Lack of clarity of the goal itself. Over time, you may realize that the goal is not clear enough to be realized.*

- *Lack of commitment to that goal. When working on it, you can come to understand that you might not truly want to achieve the goal or put in the work and time necessary.*

- *Conflicting priorities. You may come to realize that one goal is in direct conflict with another goal. The young father who wants to shoot lower scores in golf and spend time with his two infant children becomes frustrated when he can do neither and then realizes the golf game needs to be put on hold because of the time required for it.*

Goal setting works, not because of the goal itself, but due to the process and framework of setting it. It's the mental clarity and commitment the format creates that makes it work. So how do you improve discipline personally when it seems to be lacking?

Follow these four basic steps:

1. *Clarify.* Start by making sure you are really clear on what you want to accomplish. Have a vivid image in your mind of the

broad objective or outcome. If you're having trouble clarifying a picture, try stating the objective in terms of a SMART goal (Specific, Measurable, Attainable, Realistic, and Tangible). Writing it in this format, which we will cover in some depth in Chapter 7, will push you to focus on the strength and clarity of your commitment.

2. *Progress.* Focus on progress, not perfection. As you move toward the objective, you'll be tempted to try to be perfect in achieving the objective. Remember the laws of incremental improvement: You don't have to achieve your objective all at once. If you are tracking your progress, you can focus on what you've accomplished along the way, rather than how far away you are from the goal.

3. *Assess.* Keep the benefits of the objective in mind. Everyone will run into obstacles when trying to become more disciplined. It's essential to keep in mind WHY you are trying to achieve the objective and what's in it for you in accomplishing it.

4. *Enjoy.* Celebrate small wins. It's helpful to realize and reward yourself for the incremental accomplishments you've made along the way. Each small win is a step closer to your overall goals. Don't ever forget that.

These steps will work for you individually and are helpful to consider as you work with your teams. In organizations, leaders have a key responsibility to remind their people what the desired outcome is and what the benefits of the shared sacrifice or efforts to stay on task today will do for accomplishments tomorrow. Leaders make sure that they engage in these steps from a team or department standpoint just the same as if they were an individual.

What are some of the organizational aspects of discipline?

1. It starts with a clear and simple mission or purpose that communicates what's most important to the organization and why it's critical.

2. Once that is established, leaders should cascade goals and objectives that are co-designed and managed by the people who need to achieve them. Change is more readily accepted when the people impacted by it are involved in the process.

3. After that it entails efforts to provide support and feedback to stay on track. To stay disciplined, you need to constantly know whether you are on or off track so you can make the necessary adjustments.

4. Then on a day-to-day basis it's a matter of reinforcing those behaviors that best achieve those objectives and goals that everyone can commit to, and enforcing appropriate consequences when efforts fall short.

An organization should weigh the requirements of discipline so that it doesn't become constrained by blind regimentation. Many years ago, IBM was the most prestigious business-to-business information organization. They had a reputation for internal corporate discipline that transferred into positive benefits for customers. According to an interview I did with my friend, Pat Brown, who worked at IBM, although it was never written anywhere, male employees who interfaced with customers knew that their corporate culture required they wear a tie with a white shirt. If an employee showed up wearing a different colored shirt, they were chided by the rest of the team and embarrassed enough that they didn't do it again.

In this statement, IBM's founder Thomas Watson Sr. inspired the unspoken dress code: "Don't let what you're wearing distract from what you're saying." This image worked well for years until the external business environment changed and formality like white shirts went out of everyday fashion. However, IBM held on to this regimen for too long. The fact that they still wore white shirts became outside the norm and reflected that their service might not be contemporary and current. The once cutting-edge internal culture was now seen as stale and out of touch - exactly what Watson had warned against.

Many other organizations enforced discipline through certain regimentation. In my personal experiences interviewing for a position at Century 21, working at McDonalds, and chasing after Good Humor trucks, the regimentation of their strict dress codes was obvious. Century 21 required its real estate agents to wear mustard-yellow blazers to keep their brand image. McDonald's employees used to wear paper hats, and the Good Humor ice cream man wore a full uniform of all white. Now, a uniform is important when it communicates a clear message, as in the case of police officers, military, wait staff, and so on. Each organization must be very clear about the purpose of discipline and make sure it matches its overall objectives. But when it serves no purpose, it restrains and erects a barrier to new customers and recruiting efforts. The emphasis needs to remain on the discipline, not on the regimentation. Although I wore the paper hat because of its function, I would have never worked at Century 21 because I thought the mustard colored coat was uncool.

Finally, although athletes are frequently touted for having excellent discipline and provide good examples of the outcomes that discipline can provide, we should be cautious about applying their tactics to our day-to-day lives.

Typically, discipline is easier for athletes because they operate in a highly controlled environment. The outcomes they need to reach are highly tangible, and the results they achieve can be much more immediate. Essentially, they can dedicate 100 percent of their time to one singular goal. That's not necessarily the case in the work environments of the rest of us. We can become extremely frustrated trying to "be like Mike." Michael Jordan is a one in a million athlete, and his efforts toward success are nearly impossible to emulate.

The steps I've outlined here are for the rest of us. It's up to each of us to find the focus and balance between regimentation and discipline that produce the best results. Some may need a higher dosage of one or the other. It certainly should not be viewed as a one-size-fits-all proposition, but rather, as how to learn to know yourself and then determine how to best balance your discipline and your regimentation to ensure you reach and achieve your optimal level of success. The journey of success is not always an easy one, but taking the steps to remain focused on your ultimate goals and desires will certainly help you expedite the trip and reduce the obstacles along the way.

Adept in Action

- Discipline can be measured by your level of devotion to making a change. **Try this:** Do you really, really, really, really want it? List the benefits of the change to you. Make sure those benefits are strong enough for you to be motivated to act.

- Regimentation is not the same as discipline. You can be disciplined without being regimented by striving for progress not perfection. **Try this:** Instead of trying to work out every day at five a.m., you might be able to work out in the morning some days and after work others.

- Love the gap between where you are and where you want to be. **Try this:** Consider it a positive thing that you are aware of the difference and that you're working on it. Be aware of the distance you've traveled rather than the miles left to go.

- Use the power of goal setting to drive actions. **Try this:** If the goal is distant, set a broader objective and use SMART goals as incremental mileposts along the way.

- Do you want more tips and tools? **Try this:** Bookmark our website www.adeptleadership.com/tools-and-tips-adept-booksite/ to access a growing repository of valuable resources.

Chapter 5 – Authenticity

Trading in Saying for Doing

In this chapter, we'll explore the importance of authenticity in organizations. Authenticity is a buzzword in discussions about leadership, but its meaning is somewhat nebulous. What is authenticity? Is being true to yourself authentic? Is it the same as integrity? Is genuineness authentic? Dictionary.com defines authenticity as "not false or copied; genuine; real." While that may be relatively straightforward, what does authenticity mean within the context of organizations and its impact on leaders?

Are You Authentic?

From an organizational perspective, leadership cannot simply self-identify as being authentic. It is more about behavior than a state of mind. Sometimes it's hard to see our behaviors the way others may see them. We may have an intention to act one way and believe that we do. However, there is a measure of authenticity that truly resides in the eye or mind of the beholder. You may not know if you are authentic, but those around you surely have an opinion. One of my clients, a manager with a procurement team, says, "Authenticity in a leader is only recognized when the team sees the behavior, not when the leader thinks he/she is being authentic." While some other traits could be faked, like earnestness or sincerity, authenticity shines through. As Ralph Waldo Emerson said, "What you do speaks so loudly, that I cannot hear a word you say."

Although authenticity is based on other's perceptions, that does not mean it is outside of your sphere of influence. Even though it is a perception, it is based on your behavior. The challenge is not so much in being incorrectly perceived, it's in having a synchronicity between how you think and feel and how you act and engage with others.

Is Authenticity Important?

We already know that relationships are crucial to performance. Another manager I've spoken with believes this: "Authenticity is critical to leadership because now more than ever employees want to work for personal fulfillment. They need a leader who is genuine, who feels the same way about their employees as they do about completing their mission." It has been said that the millennial generation is more focused on personal fulfillment in their work than some of the preceding generations. The manager's comments speak to this aspiration.

As a leader, you can conduct yourself transactionally, trying to create situations where you can get things done. The transactional leader often uses fear or incentive to apply motivation to individuals to accomplish things. But both of those methods of motivation are externally short lived.

Types of Motivation

Fear as a motivator can work in the moment to create compliance to the job at hand. However, it doesn't allow the full potential and engagement of the individual to emerge, so a lot of energy is left on the table because of resentment or anxiety created by the fear. People exposed to fear motivation become numb to it over time, and it can lead to behavior lacking in energy and creativity. Plus, as an external force, when the fear is gone it can create a vacuum that can be filled with strong resistance and even sabotage, the opposite of the intended response. It devolves into a situation where "when the cat's away, the mice will play."

A client who is a customer support director has seen a change in how leaders approach this issue. "I have seen a transformation of leadership focus over the course of the last fifteen years in my career as a leader. The shift is to more of an authentic, accountable, transparent leader and less of a directive 'my way leader.' I believe the shift is mostly a result of how quickly organizations are forced to change course as a result of bottom line results."

Incentive motivation has limitations too. It's a kind of "this for that" approach. You try to give people something for doing what you want them to do. But this practice is also external and short lived. For example, a gift card given over the holidays for a job well done becomes an expectation during the next holiday season. If the gift card has not increased in value the next time it's given, the individual may feel as though he or she did just a so-so job. Even worse, if you do not give it at all, the employee may feel as though he or she has been punished.

Any rewards must match the needs of the specific individual. Most people don't do their work because of the incentives they receive; they do it for what those incentives intrinsically accomplish for them. It's curious to me when organizations try to reward employees with companywide, one-size-fits-all appreciation programs. When a company sends individuals on company sponsored and attended trips, or treats everyone in the rewards program the same way, they miss a fundamental element of rewards and recognition. An introvert and extrovert would respond to recognition very differently. The extrovert loves the party in their honor where they will be feted and they can celebrate with colleagues. The introvert cringes at that idea and would prefer a sign of quiet appreciation and a gift card so they can celebrate with their spouse. For the recognition or appreciation to have value, it needs to be personalized to the individual, their style, their needs, and their wants.

The most effective leaders interact transformationally, creating an environment where each individual's self-motivation is nurtured to come forward. In this environment, the relationships that the leader forges are essential to building that environment. A client who leads a team of technology specialists says, "If I develop into an authentic leader, I can better engage employees and develop employee trust. The more trust and engagement I develop, the more influential and effective I can be at navigating an organization toward its goals. I'll be better positioned to unify people toward a shared objective." The perception of authenticity from the leader remains a critical building block in creating those relationships.

For some leaders, authenticity seems more important now than ever before. An area director in engineering operations states that "people seem to value authenticity more now because of the increased amount of activity and distractions. There is so much going on and few people take the time to pay attention to what is going on right now, right in front of them." Another manager adds, "Leaders were expected to do whatever it took to reach their goals, which often came with a sense of falsehood. Employees were not always given the truth because leadership felt it might hinder their ability to get the job done." He goes on to say, "Employees were also expected to 'turn their cog' in the past, where now they are expected to contribute on a much greater level and collaborate with their colleagues to bring the whole group forward instead of just their piece."

Another leader, a regional director with a global telecommunications firm, says, "With the intense competition coupled with the emergence of social media and other forms of instantaneous communication, companies have immediate and constant feedback on how they're doing in delivering on their promise(s). They are kept in check, making authenticity a critical leadership component."

Being Genuine

Being genuine in your relationships opens the possibility that people will not like you and will not want to follow you. One manager says, "A recent theme I've seen in this view of authenticity is the concept of 'courage.' It somehow takes courage to be authentic. To be willing to reveal who you 'really' are through your words and actions." Maybe the genuine you is not an effective leader. You may possess a slew of genuine traits that don't build motivational climate.

- *You might be abrupt in speaking with people.*

- *You might be arrogant and self-important.*

- *You might be socially awkward.*

- *You might be obnoxiously self-righteous.*

If you might possess any of these traits, be aware and take action to ensure you can better tap into your genuine and authentic self. It's often said that a tiger never changes its stripes. They are what they are, and you are what you are. However, the tiger who is innately a savage beast in the wild can be trained to sit up and beg for food in the circus. Just like tigers, you can develop different attitudes and behaviors if you engage in the effort. The key: Allow yourself time to work incrementally on authenticity.

Some traits can be improved easily, while others are so deeply ingrained that they are more challenging to modify. However, through conditioning over time, most traits can be adjusted to improve effectiveness. The degree to which people need to flex their behavior will impact the amount of stress they feel while flexing.

We've observed an interesting dynamic when it comes to authenticity. Let's look at two distinct personality profiles:

- *Profile #1:* *Jan has been an operational manager with her organization for ten years. When individuals interact with her, they feel as though she does everything by the book, and her actions seem forced. She is somewhat dispassionate, and people aren't sure where they stand with her. Jan's team is long tenured and they produce at an average rate compared to their peers.*

- *Profile #2:* *Julie works in the same company in operations and has about the same tenure as Jan. She has a few quirky traits and doesn't seem to have read the book on leadership. She doesn't seem to know exactly what to do in management situations. Although she doesn't do anything illegal or disrespectful, her behavior is a little off. Julie's team gets frustrated with some of her quirky, inappropriate actions. She is very open with her team, knows their challenges, and her people say, "they always know what to expect" and "she lets them know what she wants from them." Julie's team is one of the highest producing in the company. She has received awards for the team's performance, and many of her employees have gone on to success in other departments.*

The first illustration shows that trying to be perfect in relationships at the cost of being authentic can sometimes be detrimental to your growth. Employees don't know where Jan is coming from, which has led to distrust. On the other hand, the second illustration shows that being genuine with a few flaws can draw people to you because they feel safe and know where they stand.

What's the Goal?

Part of authenticity in organizations depends on the goal. The engineering and operations director I mentioned earlier was taking a listening tour around his market, skipping his direct reports, and hosting a series of meetings where he went directly to the front lines to see what they'd have to say about the organization. He always came away with valuable insight from this exercise. He wanted to create an environment in which his people saw that he and the other leaders could be open and accepting of constructive feedback.

During one meeting, the team and some individuals seemed to have a great deal of constructive criticism. In this situation, the style of delivery and volume of comments stirred up some emotions in the director. As it continued, he got upset and thought, *I'm going to lose my temper.* He was genuinely frustrated, stressed, and angry. However, he didn't allow his genuine feeling to show. He ended the meeting and absorbed all the blows with no defensive reaction. Was he being authentic?

He came up with a critical insight when we discussed this meeting. Being authentic doesn't always mean you respond with your "natural instinct." The director felt like he was going to break down. Giving into his genuine feelings would have meant he would have lashed out. Instead, he fought the urge to do so, and he encouraged employees to share their perspectives. He knew that suppressing his real, genuine feelings would have a far greater payoff for the team and for him.

This is another reason why vision, purpose, and goals are so important in developing a motivational climate. According to one leader, "Leadership is often associated with vision, inspiration, and direction setting. However, to be successful in the long run, a leader also needs tangible results. Thus, the need to be genuine, grounded, connected to reality to be able to effectively appreciate situations, build trust, and develop realistic and smart plans."

Authentic leadership has to be measured by its results. If leadership influences people to act and be committed to doing so, then that is the overarching goal. Your degree of authenticity must help you reach those goals.

Vulnerability

In this way, authenticity and vulnerability are similar. Some vulnerability is okay, because your team may already know your strengths and weaknesses. They like to see that you have a high degree of self-awareness. Plus, your foibles can make you more approachable. However, going too far and giving too much information can be detrimental. According to a VP of operations, "My perspective at this point is that if you think being authentic is being an open book, being 'real,' sharing your true feelings and thoughts *all the time* because that is what you believe is being authentic - you will fail at being an effective leader."

Another client leader adds that "people who have been in the same leadership roles for a long time tend to struggle with finding balance between being authentic while not wanting to be seen as too vulnerable." Finding that balance between the goals of the business and the needs of your people is critical to applying authenticity for effective performance. Differentiate the two by thinking about who you are benefiting. If it's the team and your organization, you're probably on the right track. But if it's focused on you and how you feel, you may need to rethink your disclosure. Vulnerability about certain circumstances is effective, but you're not on an Oprah TV show. Be cautious about sharing too much of your personal history.

Authenticity benefits from the insight-action loop. As you work with your teams and get feedback, learn to understand the sweet spot of sharing your genuine feelings versus holding back for the good of the team and your goals. Incrementally, you can find the style that works best for you.

Finding Your Authenticity

If authenticity is incrementally built, then how do you go about erecting it? Four action steps can improve your ability to allow your genuine self to shine through. These include:

1. Insight/Awareness

2. Learning/Exposure

3. Focus/Discipline

4. Practice/Preparation

Insight/Awareness

Incremental improvement thrives on insight. It creates the constructive discontent or positive dissatisfaction with your present condition. It allows you to be aware of not only the current reality of outcomes you've produced but the gap between them and your ideal future state. One client reinforces that it begins "with becoming aware. Awareness of thought, emotion, feelings, and the physical being gives a leader critical data about their self to be able to choose the values that make up and establish a clear understanding of who the person believes they should be. A person can live without this deep understanding simply by acting and reacting as they've done their entire lives. I was this person, but I was not happy and didn't know why. Once they establish

the values, they can begin the process of checking and double checking themselves against the values to maintain the consistent behavior."

The first step in that insight: Gain an understanding and clarity
around what your authentic self looks like. Strip away the previously
developed artificial perceptions and get to the real you. In his book,
Be Yourself, Everyone Else Is Already Taken, Mike Robbins talks about
the realness that is you, not the opinions that you may espouse. It's
finding what Caroline McHugh calls "the equilibrium between self-
congratulation and self-castigation." As Robbins infers, the good news
is that no one on earth occupies this same space. Allowing yourself to
accept that fact goes a long way to finding out who you are at heart.

Once you have a sense of that true, genuine self, decide how it occupies the space in which you are operating. If your true self is angry and
bitter, you'll quickly realize it's difficult to be genuine in leadership situations. The work to change must happen at a deeply personal level.
I've consulted with people who have deep-seated issues they need to
overcome before they can improve on their effectiveness. I know this
from my own work experience.

Early on, I used to be concerned about my ability to be of assistance
and felt I might easily get in over my head and outside of my area of
expertise. I learned that my role is not to look back to assess workers' personal history and upbringing to evaluate why their issues exist.
That is the role of mental health professionals, and I am not trained
in this area. My role is to take the current situation and facilitate my
clients' efforts to move forward. Some of my clients were ready to
move forward, while others needed insight into some deeper issues
before they could make the changes necessary to improve their performance and ultimately find true authenticity.

Learning/Exposure

When you have a great sense of your true authentic self and are aware of the actions you'd like to take to improve it, you're in a great position to begin seeking the knowledge to accomplish those goals. Reading books, attending lectures, and taking classes can improve your knowledge of any subject and your understanding of those attitudes you need to develop to expedite your journey.

Becoming more authentic isn't just a mental exercise. To improve, get on the playing field. There is only so much self-work you can do in authenticity without interacting with others. The field of play in authenticity doesn't exist in a vacuum, but plays out as we associate in individual and group situations. This is the "action" of authenticity in the insight-action loop. As you engage more, you get a greater sense of how you "show up" in interactions. Gaining insight in small groups and holding each other accountable can accelerate the impact.

The director of customer support says, "Our manager, supervisory, and leadership team meets quarterly to focus on professional development. The focus of our last meeting was looking at the shadow we cast as leaders and how to improve and recognize key leadership competencies. From these conversations, we discuss and challenge each other with coaching and suggestions to improve the shadow we cast. These competencies are discussed purposefully in our weekly meetings as we continually raise the bar for our leadership team."

Focus/Discipline

Improve your authenticity by applying the ideas of focus in search of uncovering your true self. Find clarity of your purpose so you have specific guidelines on which to focus. The ability to focus on your true purpose will always help with your authenticity. It shows through without effort. When Gandhi was asked about his preferred message to the world, he said, "My life is my message." With authenticity, you can't act it, you have to be it.

Clay Christensen is an author and Harvard professor who writes and teaches about purpose. In his classic article "How Will You Measure Your Life?" he discusses how the passage of time affects people. He recounts that more and more of his college colleagues return to annual reunions "unhappy, divorced, and alienated from their children. I can guarantee you that not a single one graduated with the deliberate strategy of getting divorced and raising children who would become estranged from them. And yet a shocking number of them implemented that strategy." Christensen believes they lost focus on their overall purpose in how to live. He further illustrates his point, revealing that two of the thirty-two people in his Rhodes Scholar class subsequently spent time in jail. This was certainly not their intention in life, but, Christensen says, "Something in their lives sent them off in the wrong direction."

Without purpose, there is no authenticity. Purpose is the focus, the thing you stay devoted to. The discipline for staying on that track should have no options, no exits, and no shortcuts. The former Prime Minister of England Margaret Thatcher said it best: "Integrity has no gray."

Practice/Preparation

In employing greater authenticity, consider how to repetitiously practice it. You may stumble, you may not always be perfect, but remain dedicated so you can emerge from the process with valuable gains and better performance. The practice of authenticity leads you to realize there is always a great deal to learn. According to the VP of operations, "What I focus on is that although I have been in leadership roles for more than twenty years, I still have a lot to learn. Knowing that helps keep me authentic."

It's been said that humility is not thinking less of yourself, but thinking of yourself less. It's hard not to be humble if you are constantly learning and growing while remaining open to new ideas and concepts. Research shows this can be challenging for many leaders. A recent study by See, Morrison, Rothman, and Soll puts this in perspective. In their article "The Detrimental Effects of Power on Confidence, Advice Taking, and Accuracy," they found that powerful people are less likely to take advice from others. According to the authors, "Power elevates confidence in the accuracy of one's judgment, which in turn reduces advice taking." They go on to indicate that this mindset "could negatively affect not just advice taking, but also an individual's approach to seeking help or accepting performance feedback." Remain cautious of this as you see an increase in your personal leadership and influence within your organization.

Our experience shows that the best leaders realize good ideas and knowledge can come from anywhere and they place themselves in a position to facilitate opportunities to learn from everyone. One director adds, "Leaders need to remain open, humble, and constantly solicit and seek feedback internally with employees and externally with customers leveraging social media, surveys, 360 reviews, and other more standard types of interactive meetings (staff, skip levels, 1 on 1, etc.)."

The final component of the practice/preparation dynamic is preparing to be authentic. On the face of it, this may sound counterintuitive. "You're telling me to prepare to be genuine? To be truly real, shouldn't I just react in the moment?" Well, have your emotions ever gotten the best of you and maybe you said or did something you later regretted?

Everyone has experienced a moment where a situation or circumstance creates an environment where we are not at our best and where our actions may not represent our true self. The chances of this occurring increase if you approach the situation without a plan or have not prepared. Preparation itself can help you reconnect with your true self. This might be referred to as getting centered and remembering what your true focus is and what you are devoted to.

You can approach this preparation in many ways. Many of them work best with physical activity. Mindfulness, meditation, and exercise can all help you stay centered on your authenticity and increase your awareness of the mind/body connection. Breathing awareness and exercises can help you gain focus.

Also, you might consider your environment as a vehicle to become more centered. Decluttering your workspace, simplifying your files and systems, and removing unnecessary distractions can help you create some space and time to connect to your authentic self.

Awareness of physical limitations can help prevent a sudden shift away from your true self. Whether it's knowing what hours you work best or when you need stretch breaks, understanding how your mind and body best work is crucial to effective performance. For instance, while I am not perfect, I am mostly pleasant and positive on a day-to-day basis. But push me too many hours beyond feeding time, and I will get disagreeable. At this point, my wife would probably advise you to either give me a sandwich or run the other way.

The four items I've discussed can trigger you to find focus and remain focused so that you can connect with your true, authentic self. As you can see, being truly authentic can be challenging. However, these guidelines we've discussed and the insight we received from leaders reinforce the incremental nature of the process of becoming more authentic. It doesn't just happen overnight, but rather, as you work on increasing awareness of your true self, the greater you find that authenticity can dramatically impact your performance.

Adept in Action

- As a leader, it's crucial to act on your values and beliefs, instead of trying to be the person you think you should be. **Try this:** Develop written mission and purpose statements as your personal guide.

- At times, you may struggle to be effective and receive negative feedback on your style. **Try this:** Do some soul searching about your attitudes to isolate any barriers to your actions or behaviors.

- Awareness of your personal values and beliefs helps you become intentional about consistently applying them. **Try this:** Make sure your personal guide is written and accessible so you can revisit it periodically to ensure you're on track.

- A leader needs to stay centered and grounded around who they truly are. **Try this:** Pull out your personal guide before important meetings and challenging situations to help you get centered. Solicit insights from a close confidant to remind you of what's truly important.

- Do you want more tips and tools? **Try this:** Bookmark our website www.adeptleadership.com/tools-and-tips-adept-booksite/ to access a growing repository of valuable resources.

Chapter 6 – Influence

The Mutual Direction of Leadership

When we think of understanding leadership and exactly how we can implement ideas to incrementally improve it, it's often helpful to look back to previous experiences to analyze the difference between the fundamental truths of leadership and the myths.

Leadership Myths

Discussions about leadership often start with lists of valuable characteristics and legendary stories of leaders and what they've achieved. However, we know that techniques cannot be easily applied if habits of thought or attitudes get in the way. Sustainable change often requires a shift in mindset before tactics are valuable. Some myths of leadership create attitudinal barriers to keep us from effectively applying them to what we do.

Myth #1: You Can Only Lead at the Top - Leadership is only hierarchal and occurs from the top down. Many studies of leadership are about CEOs, heads of state, sports coaches, and others in significant roles with positional power. These people can instantly impact a wide range and great quantity of people. With their high visibility, they are the ones most studied and written about. This publicity makes it natural to consider that it's the only place where leadership occurs. However, leadership is influence or the ability to get other people to act and want to do things. Anyone can leverage their influence wherever they are. They don't have to live amongst the stars.

We all should work to move past the idea that leadership is only hierarchal and that you must be on the top of an organization or team to lead. That is simply a mindset deeply ingrained in us and really a myth at that. We can all make a difference in the cycle of leadership.

If leadership is influence, it means you can focus energy on leading regardless of your standing or stature. Consider the notion of organizational structure. Its premise: influential strength will always have more power than positional strength or power over time. Dictatorial leaders come and go as their power surges then wanes. But the power to influence incrementally is lasting and sustainable. So, the first step is believing in the possibility that you can have influence and then acting on opportunities to do so. We'll talk about this again a bit later.

Myth #2: You Are Born a Leader - Leaders are only born and not made. Sometimes tales of leadership are dramatic and become legendary. This can be a double-edged sword. These stories are inspiring, giving you hope for improvement and the belief in a brighter future. However, they also may intimidate you. They leave you feeling that a huge gap exists between the achievements of those leaders and your own personal accomplishments. Although these legendary stories about epic heroes gain the most attention, they are generally the exceptions, not the rule. Being tall, good looking, or smart are all natural-born traits. Although these might enhance your ability to lead, you can't confuse them for the leadership traits themselves.

Abraham Lincoln was not especially handsome. He was gangly and suffered from bouts of depression. Yet his thoughtful demeanor, curiosity, and ability to get to the heart of the matter greatly influenced his party, Congress, and his country. Discover your unique talents and apply them over time. Learn to become more influential. Get better at applying your influence over time. The mindset, habits, and experience of influence can be incrementally enhanced. Like anything else, there may be limitations to the height you can reach, but most leadership skills and attitudes are learned traits that can be addressed and improved.

Myth #3: You Must Command Respect and Impose Your Will - Leadership simply requires that you impose your will upon others. For whatever reason, history has glorified rushing into battle to save the day as the poster child for leadership. Parks are filled with statues of men on horseback wielding swords. That visual has become ingrained in our culture. Then we use these images as metaphors in organizational situations. We say things like "we're going to take that hill" when we're talking about achieving goals, or we're "going to war" when we're in the midst of a difficult negotiation.

Many years ago, I heard organizational consultant Meg Wheatley talk about a new paradigm for leaders. She attended a retirement party for a US Army general she knew. During the festivities, she asked him what he planned to do next. He indicated that he was going back to school to become a midwife. He wanted to help bring babies into the world. His reply surprised Wheatley. It didn't fit with the credentials of a general who had led men into battle and had overseen some of history's most significant global conflicts.

The general indicated that his plans weren't as farfetched as they seemed. He said he thought of himself as having grown and nurtured people his whole life. His response shows that the true measure of effective leadership is not so much what you do to achieve goals, but rather, what goals others achieve because of what you do.

The Tells of Leadership Success

Although the myths of leadership can restrict you and persuade you to move in the wrong direction, there is benefit in taking a historical perspective. Rather than looking at the legendary exploits of individuals and trying to relate their entire lives to what you've done, it's helpful to look at the specific characteristics of these people to discover what we can emulate. Why would looking at the past be helpful today when the world is so different than it once was?

To illustrate exactly what I mean, consider the following statements. Do these ring true for you?

- *Success and progress toward achieving your goals begins with knowing where you are going.*

- *You must possess one quality to win, and that is definiteness of purpose, the knowledge of what one wants, and a burning desire to possess it.*

- *Reduce your plan to writing. The moment you complete this, you will have given concrete form to the intangible desire.*

- *No individual has ever achieved success without others' help and cooperation.*

Do these sound particularly relevant today? My guess is you'd agree that they do. Napoleon Hill wrote these statements. In 1908, Andrew Carnegie commissioned Hill to study the great leaders of his day - people like Woolworth, Edison, Schwab, Ford, Wrigley, and Firestone. After spending almost twenty years interviewing these people and accumulating the results, Hill authored *The Law of Success* in

1928.[21] Although many characteristics of the world have dramatically changed in the last one hundred years, his statements are as true today as they were when they were first published. Why? Because they are fundamental truths about the human condition. Like other fundamental truths, these laws are timeless and relevant regardless of our own acceptance or understanding.

In many of our leadership development sessions, we ask people to list the characteristics of the most successful leaders they have ever known. The list often consists of adjectives like:

Driven
Courageous
Visionary
Collaborative
Organized
Purposeful
Planner
Focused
Disciplined
Great communicator
Influential
Motivational
Inspiring
Charismatic

Sometimes the group comes up with a longer list, sometimes a shorter one. But it almost always looks similar. There is no "reinventing the wheel," as these qualities transcend time and remain extremely important today, even though times have changed.

---

[21] Hill, Napoleon. *The Law of Success in Sixteen Lessons*. Meriden CT: Ralston University Press, 1928.

I refer to these traits as the "tells" of leadership. Like a poker player looking for signals from his opponent, these "tells" of leadership success serve as a guide for what might work for us.

The movie *The Imitation Game* provides a good example of the power of reading a tell. The year is 1939, and the British Intelligence Agency brings a mathematical genius onto their team to break the Nazi codes. The team's efforts fail until the math genius realizes that the solution is not in math or linguistics but in a common pattern embedded in every single message. Although the messages are impossible to decipher, they finally realize that the only German they need to know is "Heil Hitler." That single phrase is used in every message. The phrase is the "tell." Once they decipher the code for those two words, all the other pieces of the coded message fall into place.

Leaders may have dealt with different circumstances throughout history, but their responses always have common themes that can still be employed today. Look at just a few examples:

- *Caesar Augustus: Known as the greatest Roman Emperor, he was the founder of the Roman Empire and its first emperor. History remembers Caesar as an organizational genius. After ascending to power, he was savvy enough to create the architecture of an empire that ruled for hundreds of years. His achievements were many: consolidating power in the outlying provinces, instituting systems of census and taxation, expanding the network of roads, and founding the postal service, police, and fire departments. His ability to build these systems and processes led to unprecedented peace, or "Pax Romana," which lasted for four decades, and a political structure that survived for generations.*

- *Alexander the Great: He was a king of the ancient Greek kingdom of Macedon and became the measure against which other military leaders compared themselves. As a young boy, Aristotle mentored him in science, politics, and geography. Alexander was keenly observant. His father, King Philip, had a rambunctious horse named Bucephalus, who no one could mount or tame. He noticed that the horse seemed afraid of its shadow. But when he turned him toward the sun, Bucephalus was easy to mount and became Alexander's faithful steed. He was also unconventional. A man named Gordius had tied his cart to a pole outside the temple to appease the god Zeus with a very intricate knot. Tradition held that whoever untied the knot would conquer all of Asia. When Alexander came upon the challenge, he tried unsuccessfully to untie the Gordian knot. After several attempts, he became frustrated and sliced it in half with his sword, proclaiming, "It makes no difference how they are loosened." He was immediately hailed as the leader that had outsmarted the ancient puzzle with his "out of the box" thinking.*

- *Joan of Arc: From the Lorraine region of France, Joan was "pulled" by visions and said she heard voices that told her to deliver her country from the English. She is considered the youngest person in history to command the armies of a nation. Her influence and resilience were substantial. Even after being injured on the battlefield, she continued to fight. She is also known to have courage in her convictions, sticking to her beliefs even when she was accused of being a witch and despite the threat of death and her eventual demise by being burned at the stake.*

- *George Washington: The first president of the United States and one of its founding fathers. Few people know George lost more battles than he won. He demonstrated great perseverance while also unifying the United States as the only president in history to be unanimously elected president twice. George was always open to the advice of others. He established the concept of the presidential Cabinet as he sought a variety of perspectives. He always demonstrated integrity and self-control. Although not perfect, he strove to be virtuous. He realized that as president, everything he did created a precedent for the future. "I walk on untrodden ground. There is scarcely any part of my conduct which may not hereafter be drawn into precedent." He relinquished power when most men strove for it, stepping down as commander in chief in 1783 and declining a third term. He expected no political or financial reward. Thomas Jefferson believes Washington's behavior probably prevented the American Revolution from devolving into chaos, creating a strong foundation for "liberty to continue."*

Here are some other significant historical figures along with the characteristics they were known for:

Mahatma Gandhi - learned from mistakes, forgiveness, faith in himself

Mother Teresa - gracious, determined, humane, convicted

Nelson Mandela - tenacity, self-awareness, sense of humor

Martin Luther King Jr. - vision, passion, bravery

Although these leaders demonstrated tremendous influence, another aspect of leadership is essential to mention here. Whenever we discuss leadership, look beyond the individual characteristics to the overall sum of a person's efforts and impact on others.

In addition, be cautious about worshipping leaders as heroes and attempting to live like any one of these individuals. No one is perfect, not even the amazing leaders mentioned above. For example, Caesar Augustus had a reputation as a thug while he strategically navigated his way to the top. And Alexander the Great was said to have been ruthless and brutal and an excessive drinker, dying at age thirty-three due to complications from an all-nighter.

Ultimately, we must measure the effectiveness of leaders with a moral or ethical compass. That may be even more important than their traits alone. Some frequently mention Adolf Hitler as one of the greatest leaders of our time when referring to *just* individual characteristics (and not positive or negative impact on society). He certainly shared many characteristics of successful leaders. However, we can't consider these traits in a vacuum. Perfection is impossible to attain, but the impact of influence on humanity must be considered. In that light, we can never suggest that Hitler was in any sense of the word a great leader. He forever stained society. He used his strong leadership qualities to create great pain and suffering.

As you consider any study of leadership or review of models of leadership, remember that no one person possesses all the traits to be an effective leader. Finding your unique leadership style is an intimate and individual process. To become a great leader, do it for yourself and rely on your own special skillset. Avoid letting the myths affect your attitude about leadership. Leverage your strengths to begin to lead from where you are.

Although these categories can help you become a better leader, ultimately, we're looking to debunk one of the biggest myths outlined in success literature: the concept that there are "secrets" of success. As I've tried to illustrate in this book, there really are no secrets. These ARE the steps, these ARE the traits, and these ARE the skills. The challenge isn't in *knowing* what they are, it's in the *doing*.

We can all learn to apply the principles of success and leadership if we work on them incrementally. Let's look at ways to do that.

The Two-Way Street of Leadership

When we speak of leadership, we are really talking about influence. Influence doesn't happen without proper communication. Remember, communication is the connection demonstrated in this formula:

a message sent = a message received

The critical component of this equation is the equal sign. That sign means effective communication occurs when each individual is responsible for one part of the process and makes sure it happens. Although the equation is simple, getting to the equal sign is complex. Effective communication doesn't exist without information flow, the back and forth of statements, attempts at clarification, active listening, and readjustment of message. The most influential people know that this is truly a two-way street. They know they can't learn about the challenges and obstacles others face if they view it as a one-way-only process.

Positional leaders who don't listen to their people are doomed to fail because they aren't as engaged with the customer condition as are the people on the front lines. Conversely, if people on the front lines don't leverage their influence, they are subconsciously sabotaging the impact and effectiveness of the goals the organization is trying to accomplish.

As mentioned in Myth #1, we can't just think of leadership as a top down process. We need to think about leadership at all levels. If leadership is about influencing others to achieve goals and having them *want* to do so, this can be achieved at every level of the organization. Leaders with positional power can motivate people to comply to do things and reach targets just because of their positional or hierarchical authority. The most effective leaders make this a two-way street by creating a motivational climate for individuals to fully engage in the process of achieving their goals.

This requires leadership from the hierarchical subordinates as well. They must show more initiative and take greater responsibility. They should stick their neck out to communicate disagreement. They must make suggestions and step forward when asked. If leadership is influence, then individuals at all levels must take personal responsibility for their part in acting effectively.

We have all worked with organizations that have had a dictatorial-type manager. They lead through positional power, providing strict direction on what to do, when to do it, and how it should be done. They leave very little to the creativity and initiative of the individuals who follow. It's a real "my way or the highway" situation. When a more empowering leader replaces that individual, often we've seen an interesting phenomenon occur. The new leader finds that when he talks about getting people involved, and creates situations for people to be engaged, they don't step up, even though a positive shift in leadership recently has occurred.

In the movie *The Shawshank Redemption*, Red, played by Morgan Freeman, discusses a phenomenon in prison that mirrors this leadership situation. Describing the barriers in the prison, he says, "These walls are funny. First you hate 'em, then you get used to 'em. After long enough, you get so you depend on 'em. That's institutionalized." He is describing the outcome of a dictatorial leader on his/her organization. Employees can grow so accustomed to being told what to do and how to do it that they expect it to happen and can't react any other way.

When James Whitmore's character, Brooks, is released from prison and is so unnerved by his newfound "freedom" that he takes his own life. Leaders who are replacing a dictatorial type leader must realize that they must incrementally create the new climate. They must give their people time to adjust to the new circumstances. At the same time, the subordinates need to realize that change has come and start taking initiative and speaking up when the opportunity arises.

A two-way approach to leadership is more like a rope than a pathway. The leader can offer the rope to the people, but the rope cannot be pushed to them. Rather, both sides must grab it. The formal leader offers the rope, and the informal leader must take hold. To accomplish this goal, employees can show leadership within organizations in different ways:

- *Take Personal Responsibility. Employers want employees who take responsibility for their actions, good or bad. They want employees to understand their roles in outcomes that are positive and negative and are willing to solve problems on their own.*

- *Be a Team Player. A recent survey of more than fifteen hundred CEOs indicated that one of the greatest human capital needs is not subject matter expertise. It is the capability to work in collaboration with others. The future of work is more and more about working collectively to tap different skills and attitudes and the diversity of thought that's available.*

- *Communicate Effectively. With the fast-paced world of constant connection and information flow, pressure on effective communication is greater than ever. Employees need to listen, write, and speak with clarity and purpose to save time and reduce errors.*

- *Assume Greater Responsibility. Employers want people who show initiative and are willing to step up. They look for people who act like owners of the organization even if their names are not on the wall.*

- *Manage Multiple Priorities. Most modern workflow isn't sequential but a series of leapfrogging events where other people's actions must fill in pieces before you can continue on your path. Employees need to handle this workflow pattern while focusing on what matters most every day.*

When employees take these steps, they can show leadership no matter their formal role in the organization hierarchy.

Leaders Among Us

The most effective leaders empower others to reach a greater level of their true potential. In organizations, great leaders achieve an organization's goals by creating an engaged workforce. A leader should be considered great if he or she can groom a group of successors who can be as good - if not better than - they were. For the most effective leaders, one measure of their effectiveness is not only what they did while they were in charge, but what sustained success they leave behind as a legacy.

To create engaged teams, the ones comprised of fully committed employees, leaders need to take four definitive steps:

1. Share information widely

2. Create opportunities for participation and contribution

3. Remove obstacles from making progress

4. Define the meaning of the work

Step #1: Share Information Widely - Leaders who share information widely are seen as transparent and open. This builds trust with their teams because people feel there aren't any hidden agendas. Plus, when people feel as though they are "in the know," they feel more connected to the objectives and motivated to achieve them. In addition, by sharing information, the leader communicates what's most important to them so people know the key priorities they need to focus on.

Step #2: Create Opportunities for Participation and Contribution - As we stated, in organizational development, people are more committed to those aspects of business they participate in creating. Leaders who get their people involved early in change initiatives gain greater commitment to those initiatives even when they move in different directions than originally suggested. People don't need to have all their ideas accepted, they just want to feel as though they were heard and their contribution mattered.

Step #3: Remove Obstacles from Making Progress - When you are lucky enough to observe a great leader personally, the impact is unforgettable. This is true of my experience with Roger Oxendale, the founding president of Nemours Children's Hospital in Orlando. He consistently introduced himself in employee gatherings and community events by stating his name and saying that *he* was there to serve *them*. Imagine the power of a servant leader who walked his talk at every opportunity and led by example, right down to picking up litter in the hallway or stopping to chat with associates in their workspace - someone who really listened to their challenges, rather than hiding in their office in the "C-suite."

When leaders see themselves in a support role, they can help their people by making them more likely to accomplish the things that need to get done and inspire them to go further than they thought they could. When people aren't making progress, they get frustrated and feel dissatisfied. Rather than piling on busywork and requiring unnecessary reporting, an effective leader can act as a filter to make sure nonessential issues don't get in the way of employees achieving their objectives.

Step #4: Define the Meaning of Work - People at all levels are more engaged in activities when their work has a bigger meaning than the task or job itself. Some occupations easily translate to significant purpose. Nurses and doctors, for example, save lives every day. However, some members of nonclinical support teams rarely interact with a patient. So, it's incumbent upon the leader to make sure all members of the team know how their job responsibilities contribute to saving lives too and how their daily work supports the overall purpose of the organization.

By reinforcing these four steps, leaders influence their team to live in a culture where these actions are the norm rather than the exception and become an expectation for all employees. In addition, by employing these steps, they also create plenty of opportunities for informal leaders to emerge and demonstrate their influence and the impact it can have on the team's results. Finally, focusing on these steps provides a format for training on those factors that are critical to creating a culture of commitment. This reinforces and sustains that culture.

Becoming a Better Leader

So, the question remains: how do I use these ideas to find my unique path to becoming a better leader?

Instead of worshipping the leadership legends as heroes and mirroring their entire personas, we can incorporate certain characteristics and ultimately find the ones that are right for our own specific scenarios. Whenever you're looking at a wide range of traits and options that seem to be overwhelming in scope, break them down into smaller usable pieces.

To provide some guidance for finding the path that's right for you, we've created a framework to draw upon. It's an interrelated group of characteristics that let you look at your traits and see how you can enhance them. The framework is ADEPT Leadership®. ADEPT is an acronym that attempts to sum up many of these characteristics into usable attributes.

These attributes are:

A - Awareness

Great leaders maintain high levels of awareness in three critical areas.

1. **Self.** Knowing your strengths and individual challenges is critical to being able to influence others and multiply your activities.

2. **Others.** Leaders are keenly aware of the motivations and skills of those around them and how they impact performance.

3. **Environment.** Leaders scan their environment to better understand the impact elements have on their current and future results.

D - Direction

Leaders are usually very clear and focused on where they are going themselves. They are also capable of promoting a clear, concise, and compelling direction to others.

E - Execution

Influence works when it generates action. Leaders must produce results to maintain credibility and sustain personal and organizational growth.

P - People Centric

Leaders have a focus on getting things done through others and understanding what it takes to do so. They seem less focused on things and more focused on the people that do those things.

T - Talent Management

The most effective leaders maximize the potential of their people. They seem to get more engagement from others. Many people vividly remember leaders who believed in them before they believed in themselves.

Although we offer comprehensive training programs that help participants apply the attributes listed above in their day-to-day work, there is too much in the model to thoroughly cover here. However, you can use this model as a guide to clarify some of your leadership strengths and better begin to understand some areas of improvement.

As we consider becoming a more adept leader, remember that there are universal principles of leadership and that there are no secret traits. Great leaders provide opportunities for growth and development on the two-way street of leadership. Great employees seize the opportunity to learn and grow and understand that they can influence others no matter what their formal authority is.

When the two-way street is open and clear with information flowing back and forth, it acts as a wide boulevard on the road to organizational success. When the influence boulevard is wide, the organization is head and shoulders above its competition and heading in the direction of maximizing its potential.

Adept in Action

- Living up to mythical leadership ideals can be overwhelming. **Try this:** Spend some time in self-study to clarify what your strengths are in conjunction with the needs of your position. Create a plan to develop them.

- You don't need positional power to make an impact. Leadership and influence can be learned if you don't limit your beliefs about your role. **Try this:** Take personal responsibility regardless of your position. Focus on what you can impact by setting goals and taking action in areas that are within your influence.

- Leaders must create commitment, not just compliance. **Try this:** Practice sharing information, creating opportunities for participation and contribution, removing obstacles from your people who are making progress, and defining the meaning of the task at hand.

- The ADEPT model (Awareness, Direction, Execution, People-Centric Attitudes, and Talent Management) allows you to see if you are having all the influence you can. **Try this:** Review the definitions and consider how you are living each of the attributes. Develop action steps to improve in each area.

- Do you want more tips and tools? **Try this:** Bookmark our website www.adeptleadership.com/tools-and-tips-adept-booksite/ to access a growing repository of valuable resources.

Chapter 7 – Implementation

Reliable Practices for Effective Transformation

In the early '80s, the food company Campbell hired Howard Moskowitz to improve the sales of Prego spaghetti sauce. The company asked him to make the perfect sauce that everybody would love. Through extensive research, Moskowitz found there was no one perfect spaghetti sauce, but there were really good sauces - plural. Individual tastes vary tremendously. What one person considers to be good can be very different than another. He discovered that one sauce will not satisfy all people, but a product line of a few different sauces could satisfy many. To make progress, Campbell concluded that the perfect sauce was unattainable, and the company adjusted its plan. [22] It moved away from perfection for all, which could not be achieved, to the effectiveness for many, which was doable.

Customize Change

The concept of moving away from perfection toward doable effectiveness can be applied to improving personal effectiveness and increasing success. Here's the basic incremental development principle: focus

---

[22] Gladwell, Malcolm. "Transcript of "Choice, happiness and spaghetti sauce"." Malcolm Gladwell: Choice, happiness and spaghetti sauce - TED Talk Subtitles and Transcript - TED.com. Accessed May 01, 2017. https://www.ted.com/talks/malcolm_gladwell_on_spaghetti_sauce/transcript?language=en.

on your own path to growth and development and find the tools that work best for you that you can implement. The implementation of that method - not the idea or method you choose to follow - is what's important. For example, your best exercise equipment is the one you work out on, not the treadmill you hang your coats on or the bike collecting dust in the corner.

Remember, implementation through incremental improvement is key.

Goals are one of the most effective tools to assist with incremental improvement. Goal setting is a methodology that has been proven through extensive research to improve performance. According to Edwin Locke, who has studied goal setting for more than forty years, "Goals affect performance by directing attention, mobilizing effort, increasing persistence, and motivating strategy development." Most people know about and understand the idea of setting goals. However, in our work coaching thousands of individuals in goal setting, we have found that most people don't really apply the idea for maximum effect. Ask people about personal goals, and many will say they believe in goals. Ask the same people if they have goals, and a few will say they do. When they are asked if they achieve their goals regularly, only a handful will say yes.

Use a Process

To make goals work incrementally, the whole goal setting process must be adequately applied. What follows this paragraph is the methodology we teach to make sure you are using the power of goals to maximum advantage. Most people's first mistake: they are vague about their goals. They say things like "become a better leader," "get in better shape," or "work better with my team." These are all positive things to aspire to, but they are not goals. They are just phrases based on an idea or desire without the person thoroughly thinking about what they want to achieve on a deeper, clearer, and committed level. We believe only statements that live up to the SMART acronym are really goals. (Specific, Measurable, Attainable, Realistic, ~~Tangible)~~ Time-oriented

Once the statement is converted into this format, it becomes a goal. However, the conversion process is not always easy. It takes time to boil ideas down to their essence. In assisting people with making their aspirations SMART, we've found it valuable to focus on what happens as result of their effort in two ways:

- *An outcome achieved*

- *A behavior or action consistently realized*

Many people struggle with goals because of previous conditioning about what a goal should be. We hear that you should set your goals high and reach for the stars. We hear about Big Hairy Audacious Goals. These are good ideas as dreams, desires, or aspirations, but are often stated as such large or broad concepts that people don't know what action to take or behavior to change to act on them. Aspirations are great for creating a vision, but sometimes they are too far off in the future to clarify in SMART format. However, at some level they need to be clarified in order to benefit from the motivational power of the SMART format.

Progress, Not Perfection

People also fall into the will and determination challenge trap. Some-one finally gets the idea to work on an issue and set a goal. Because they are suddenly motivated, they plan on doing the activity from this day forward. They start down the path believing they can do it perfectly from now on.

A manager decides he's finally going "to get his act together" and start planning his workday before he gets started in the morning. He comes in on Monday morning and takes ten minutes to create and prioritize a list of things he needs to accomplish before he starts doing any work. His day goes well, and he thinks planning really does help. The next day he comes in and plans again. On the third day, he takes his son to school and gets in a little later, and because things are busy he forgets his planning time. The next day he is stuck in traffic and has an early appointment that he just gets to in time, so he skips his planning time. When he comes in on Friday, he's disappointed that he's already missed two days from his goal of planning every day. He skips planning that day so he can start fresh on Monday to try, once again, to plan every day.

The problem here: from the start, the manager focuses on perfection rather than clarifying what it's like at the finish. The R of SMART comes into play here. It's not realistic to believe you can plan every day if you haven't been planning at all. It's a brand-new habit, and you must realize it takes time to change a habit. Although it may be "attainable" to achieve a goal, it may not be "realistic" based on where you are. Think about it in sports terms: the goal is to ensure the ball or the puck crosses the line. It doesn't matter where it starts. Goals must focus on when the process target is reached, not where it starts. Every day, work up to reaching your goal incrementally, not all at once. If you're focused clearly on the end, it's much easier to strive for progress rather than perfection.

Making the conversion from a broad phrase to a SMART goal assures that the statement isn't a throwaway that leads to useless effort, frustration, and stress. If a statement can be placed in the SMART format, it is a measure of the clarity one has around that goal and the commitment to accomplishing it.

Test Your Objective

When converting an aspiration into a goal, make sure it's really something worthwhile to do. To ensure that, consider the following format that "tests" the value of doing in three ways:

The Benefit Test

What benefit do you gain by accomplishing this objective? Why do you really, really, really want it? Your reasons should be logical *and* emotional. You must feel strongly enough about them that they will help you overcome challenges.

We had a client who had struggled with her stated goal of "losing weight" for years. We'll call her Sarah. During a training session, I asked Sarah how losing weight would benefit her. She said, "Better health, greater happiness, and longer life." I told her those statements didn't sound like her goals but something someone else might say to her. They were more of a cliché than something that really meant something to her personally. I thought her statement needed more work, but she went away thinking that she had finally got it.

The Challenge Test

Often, we are aware of the potential challenges we face before we even start trying to accomplish an objective. This test allows you to be up front with those potential challenges and attempt to be proactive in solving them.

A couple of weeks later, Sarah came back. I asked how she was progressing toward her goal. She said she wasn't making any progress; in fact, things were getting worse. She explained her challenges in losing weight. "I like to eat whatever I want, I don't like to work out, and I don't like to sweat." I agreed that those were substantial obstacles. Again, I asked Sarah about the benefits she would realize in meeting her goal. She repeated her mantra, *"Better health, greater happiness, and longer life."* I suggested that those generic benefits were not strong enough to overcome her obstacles. They didn't carry enough weight. I asked her to think about why she really, really, really, wanted to lose weight - to think about it more deeply to see if she could uncover the real answer. And to pass the benefit test.

Two weeks later, Sarah returned excitedly. She happily disclosed that she had lost a couple of pounds. "What changed?" I asked her. She said she had discovered why she really, really, really wanted to lose weight. Sarah said that she made a lot of presentations to high-powered boards of directors and community leaders. Whenever she was a little overweight, she felt self-conscious and thought the board didn't respect her as much as when her weight was more in control. She said that, for her, gaining and keeping respect was the real benefit of losing weight. When she realized that, she finally had the energy and motivation to devise a plan that worked for her. Sarah was now excited about considering what she would eat and being more mindful of it. Because she didn't like to sweat, she started walking, an exercise that would help her get fit but not sweaty. Clarifying the true benefit of weight loss to her helped Sarah overcome the challenges of becoming leaner.

The Participant Test

Sometimes we can't accomplish goals by ourselves and need help from others. Who do you need for support, for information, for resources? In addition, for personal goals, remember that we are all more willing to break commitments to ourselves than to other people. Who can help hold you accountable?

Sarah made pretty good progress, but despite her efforts and newfound focus, sometimes she skipped walking "because it becomes kind of boring." One day, she asked a friend to walk with her. This added accountability because they both had to get up early to make it happen. Plus, the time flew by as they talked the whole way, which made walking much more interesting and enjoyable.

* * *

I've been told one of the hardest things to give up is smoking. Recently, a client told me about an experience she had that illustrates and reinforces the power of the participant test. We will call the client Amy.

One morning as Amy prepared for work, she reached for her cigarettes from their usual perch near her keys. The pack wasn't there. She couldn't find it anywhere. Finally, she asked her seven-year-old son about it. He said he had thrown it away because he didn't want to see her get sick. She became angry and lashed out at him for touching things that weren't his. On her way to work, she realized that her young son was just trying to help. She felt horrible for how she had reacted. It gnawed at her all day. When she returned home, she spoke with her son during dinner about how bad she felt. She apologized to him for how she had treated him when he was being so considerate.

After dinner, he said he would wait for her while she had her usual night-time smoke outside. She told him that she wasn't going outside and that she was going to try to stop smoking. He looked at her with a big smile and ran to hug her. "This is the best day EVER!" he exclaimed. Up until that point, she hadn't committed to quit and wasn't even sure that she could. Whenever she thought about having a cigarette after that, remembering his reaction reinforced her resolve. The thought of her son's happiness and his look of joy when he believed she'd be quitting the smoking habit prevented her from lighting up.

You see, it's often easy to break the commitments we make to ourselves. No one ever knows that you want to be a better communicator at work or begin an exercise program if you keep it to yourself, so you can let it slide more easily. Most people don't want to let other people down, especially those who care for them, so we will take action if we state our goals to another person.

Be Clear

Benefit, Challenge, and Participant Tests can help you evaluate whether you are truly clear about and committed to your goals. Some people can do this entire process informally in their minds. It just seems intuitive and natural. They can get very clear on what they want to achieve, become completely committed to it, and stay focused on what they want regardless of circumstances.

For the rest of us inundated by distractions and overarching shifts in priorities, it can be extremely beneficial to work through these guidelines to gain clarity into what we really want and to discover if the benefits are worth the effort. Without specific goals, we make vague statements to ourselves that can lead to stress from not knowing what truly needs to be done and frustration from not achieving what we want.

When we train ourselves in this incremental process, our goal setting becomes a tool. The power of goals is in the specificity to generate our internal motivation and drive to focus our energy on the achievement.

How Companies Implement Improvement

Organizations can apply this idea culturally by clarifying aspirational objectives, the benefits of which are clear and compelling to employees. This would allow managers to set SMART goals for their teams that can pass the three tests and then become incremental goals. After that, the organization can apply tracking methods to display progress toward those goals. This allows individuals to keep the goals in front of them and see their incremental progress. This motivates individuals and allows for actions and efforts to be corrected before they are too far off track.

Goals can also help clarify the requirements for the job. These requirements must consider the technical skills needed for the job as well as the human relationship elements. Often, organizations seem to accept these on an either/or basis. They justify the decision because that individual is so valuable on the one trait and the other trait is deemed less important. This is most frequently seen with highly technical employees who don't have the people skills to interact effectively with their colleagues. Sometimes, companies will justify bad behavior because of the genius technical skills these people bring to the organization. However, they need to consider the impact of the poor people skills and the exponential impact that behavior has on the rest of the team. In many cases, when these individuals have been removed from the situation, the company finally sees the true impact of the negative behavior and realizes that the depth and scope of that impact is far greater than the positive impact of the technical skills. There is no such thing as "half" an employee. You are paying good money for their efforts, so you should realize full benefit.

Organizations must practice the fundamental principle of change, understanding that people are more committed to things they participate in creating. To reduce resistance and increase buy-in, they should employ processes to ensure that those who are most closely affected by changes have an opportunity to be involved in them. Even when employee suggestions are not implemented, they will commit to the change if they feel as though their opinion has been heard.

What Can Leaders Do?

In any implementation, there is always a need for correction if methods need to be modified and recognition of outcomes are achieved. Surprisingly, a vacuum of interaction exists when it comes to providing feedback. The ability to provide clear, direct, and helpful feedback is critical to effective leadership. It is the skill most often underutilized by leaders.

There is almost an epidemic of leaders not providing valuable feedback for their direct reports. This may not be so surprising when we look at the current state of cultural discourse, as we certainly don't have many role models for constructive conversations and civil disagreement. The airwaves are filled with talk shows that feature people arguing with, talking over, yelling at, and disrespecting each other. That seems to be the model for dialogue we've grown to understand and copy.

Leaders need to break this mold by modeling how people can have constructive conversations. They need to take the lead on providing effective feedback to employees at all levels, whether that be for delivering positive reinforcement for a job well done or for negative consequences and constructive criticism for actions and behavior that are off the mark. Leaders who give feedback well usually have the most effective teams. The team members know where they stand and understand what's expected of them. They don't need to wait for formal annual reviews because they already know what they need to address and improve. Typically, they are more engaged in their work because expectations are clear.

Leaders who provide more consistent and effective feedback have less grievances and long-term conflict with employees because they create an environment where employees are required to address issues before they become too big and overwhelming.

Keys to Providing Feedback

Usually, you decide it's time to give feedback because of some emotional trigger. The employee has been late one too many times, they have been disrespectful once again, or made the same error over and over. The emotion generates the desire to finally act, to "put my foot down." Here's what you must remember about giving feedback: you must separate the trigger for taking the action from the method of providing the feedback itself. The emotion may generate the initiative, but it's not the way to deliver it. Instead, use a framework to create a method to provide feedback more effectively.

Four critical characteristics of providing effective feedback are:

1. *Descriptive* - Not judgmental. Saying that it was a "sloppy" job doesn't help the individual understand what they need to fix. Telling someone they did "great" doesn't clarify what they did that was effective so they can repeat it in the future. Be specific about actions or outcomes. Sloppy becomes "over a dozen grammatical errors, seven typos, inconsistent formatting." A great job is more like, "You handled a difficult customer with grace. You assured and validated their concerns and provided beneficial alternatives." In both scenarios, it's easy for the receiver to know what your expectations were and to focus on the behavior to either fix or repeat the actions they took.

2. *Appropriate* - Delivered at the right time and circumstances. Feedback is typically most effective when it's delivered in proximity to the action that created the opportunity for feedback as long as you're thoroughly thinking through the process logically, not emotionally. It's also important to be intentional about the circumstances. Most constructive feedback should be delivered in private. Like the old saying goes, "Praise in public, punish in private." There are, however, times when constructive criticism needs to be delivered to an individual in a public setting. If the behavior has violated the values or ethics of the group, the behavior really needs to be called out. If not, the lack of feedback

in the group setting can send the message that the behavior is acceptable.

3. *Actionable* - Within the receiver's ability to control. It isn't realistic to believe that providing feedback on something outside of the receiver's influence will have any impact. Feedback given in this way could create confusion and frustration. Although it's said that what gets measured gets done, that only works if the individual can control it.

4. *Accurate* - Must be the truth about the circumstance. Constructive feedback can seriously harm a relationship if the feedback is not accurate. Inaccurate positive feedback - "You're the best singer ever" - can create a false sense of confidence or reduce the credibility of the giver. If the feedback is based on hearsay, it can jeopardize the relationship and reduce the impact of any feedback given in the future.

These aren't complex ideas, yet they are nearly impossible to remember when you are in an emotional state. You need to drill them into your head and be prepared. You can use these characteristics to frame the conversation, clarify the real issue, and be confident that the issue is worth addressing in the first place.

If you incorporate these elements, you will most likely be more confident in providing the feedback. You will come across as interacting in your more natural style. This will make the receiver much more comfortable. This will make them much more receptive and less defensive about what you have to say.

Becoming ADEPT

The key to the first step in becoming more ADEPT, as discussed in Chapter 6, resides in the first word of the acronym. Awareness is a critical piece of incremental improvement. You need to understand where you are and where you are coming from before you can set a path to improvement. Your smartphone can give you directions to your destination only if your location service is turned on. Awareness is like turning on your current location. It's important to understand any gap between where you are and where you want to be. Consider these two basic components of awareness:

- *Things you want to do*

- *Things you want to be*

Oftentimes, one of the gaps between what you want to do and what you're currently doing is in who you are. Sometimes you need to consider who you want to be or become before you can achieve certain objectives. If you want to communicate better (doing) you may need to focus on being more patient. If you want to make sure your team understands what you want them to do the first time, you may need to become more specific in your requests. These two components are linked, and one can support the other. If a person wants to become a better listener, they can focus on counting to five after someone finishes talking (doing). Over time, they may realize that they have become a better listener.

As your awareness increases, keep a perspective on where you are. Many organizations use 360-degree surveys with leaders to understand the perspective others have on their leadership skills and habits. Frequently, I tell clients that many of us have an inkling that we aren't perfect, and the 360 survey results prove that we're right.

The most critical part of the 360 process is the leaders' perspective about the information they receive and how they react to it. When they recognize the gap between where they are and where they'd like to be, they must deal with their dissatisfaction positively. Rather than lamenting what they are not, they can more clearly see their strengths and understand their challenges so they know what they may need to work on.

Investors call the perspective on the gap "constructive discontent," the ability to see shortcomings and rather than thinking negatively, considering how things can be done better. This is a critical mindset for successful implementation of appropriate actions when your self-awareness increases.

Because awareness precedes change, how do you become more aware? You need to learn and listen.

- *Learning* - *Learn about your environment, critical components of your work, best practices for performance, industry standards, or other aspects that can impact your performance. Compare what you've learned to your current practices and see if any opportunities for adjustment and improvement exist.*

- *Listening* - *Listen to what others think and feel. Try to understand by asking effective questions and postponing judgment until you are perfectly clear. Seek out insight about your performance from others. Use assessments and tools like 360 reviews to get others' perspectives. When combined with your own experience, listening and truly understanding others can be a valuable tool in uncovering areas of improvement.*

Another key to long-term incremental improvement is to truly get in the mindset that it IS a journey, not a destination. Focus on progress, not perfection. My cousin Al taught me this rhyme. He didn't' make it up but put his own spin on the original by St. Jerome, and it has stuck with me through the years: *"Good, better, best, never let it rest 'til your good becomes your better, and your better is your best."*

This brings to mind the idea of progression, or a succession of events. Incremental improvement can be thought of as this succession. We are always in a process of evolution. The late Muhammed Ali, one of the most well-known humans of our era, said, "If a man believes the same things at fifty that he did at twenty, he's wasted thirty years." Our evolution is an ongoing event and is a part of our personal succession to the next level of realizing our true potential.

A more traditional organizational definition of succession is in the planning of transfer of leadership. But this shouldn't be just a top-level activity with executives and those who reside in the C-suite. This is a crucial role for leaders at all levels because they usually can't advance if they don't have a replacement. Developing a bench should be on the mind of any leader. Working toward this goal empowers others to seek more responsibility and expand the scope of their influence. It also helps build organizational capacity as more people are ready for transition into other roles. Finding, developing, and nurturing your replacement is the ultimate role of a leader. Think of this as multiplying yourself. As we scan the landscape of successful leaders, their legacy of developing other leaders is a true measure of their success.

How do you develop other leaders?

- *Help Them See What They Don't. As we've mentioned, awareness is critical to growth. Awareness must be self-realized, and people must reach it through their perspective, not yours. Constantly provide feedback to help them reach that self-awareness. Asking appropriate and probing questions goes a long way to helping them increase their personal understanding as opposed to strict judgment and evaluative lecturing.*

- *Provide Boundaries for Expectations. All employees are owed clarification about their roles and responsibilities and in understanding their workplace and the scope of the field of play. As opposed to being constrained by deeply detailed and restrictive steps, boundaries allow for creativity and flexibility to be employed to come up with more effective decisions and problem solving.*

- *Define the Level of Support and Resources They Require. Clarify with each employee the support they feel they require and the tools and processes they feel they need to be successful. Provide authority levels that match their responsibility to ensure that what they are capable of doing can be implemented in the team or workgroup.*

- *Provide Constant and Effective Feedback. All people do better when they receive effective feedback. It's said that when performance is measured, it gets done, and when it's measured and feedback is given, it gets done at a higher rate. Although much time is often spent with low performers to get them up to speed, remember that high performers thrive because performance tweaks can take them to the next level.*

- *Share Your Stories. My daughter gave me a lesson in this area. We were having a typical discussion that included some advice about what she should do to make a particular decision. I was going through my "consulting thing," asking her a series of questions to help her come to her own conclusion. Finally, in exasperation, she said, "From now on, when I ask you for advice, I don't want you to ask me questions. I want you to tell me what you'd do, and then I'll weigh that with the other advice I'm getting and make my own decision." As a leader, accept the fact that your way is not the only or most valuable way, but that it can significantly contribute to the perspective, problem solving, and decision-making process of the other person. Also remember that storytelling is a powerful influencer because it allows you to illustrate a perspective or concept without making it personal.*

- **Give Them Stretch Assignments.** *We all know someone who believed in us before we believed in ourselves. I'll never forget working with my older brother, John, on remodeling his house. I was just a boy at the time. I hadn't had much experience working on projects around my own house beyond watching my dad do it. On his project, my brother encouraged me to help him do the bulk of the work and use tools I had never used. He helped increase my awareness of what it took to do this type of work and gave me the confidence to know I could accomplish it. As a leader, you can demonstrate your confidence in people by providing them with an opportunity to do something that might be on the edge or even beyond their current capabilities. Your faith will create or renew their confidence to do the job, and that success will impact them in future opportunities well after that job is finished.*

The gains or improvements we make are impacted by our perspective in looking at them. Most people want to see immediate improvements and get impatient if things don't change quickly. Their perspective is short term, and their focus is on the here and now. An incremental perspective focuses on the outcome. With a clarity of what the goal will look like when it's accomplished, it's easier to allow for the ups and downs and imperfections that typically come from trying to achieve something new. This perspective also allows for appreciation of the process to get there and the benefit of feedback and correction along the way. Incremental changes can be as transformational and dramatic as sudden change. The only difference is the perspective in looking at them. Remember the bonsai!

Adept in Action

- Goal setting is a key lever to making incremental improvement. **Try this:** Translate a broad objective into a SMART goal that is clear and that you are committed to.

- Taking the time in planning a goal goes a long way to achieving it. **Try this:** Make sure you answer what's in it for you to achieve the goal, what are the challenges you'll face, and what are the support and participation you'll need to accomplish it.

- When your people achieve goals, or fall short, provide feedback. **Try this:** Wait until strong emotions about the issue have subsided, then take a few moments to formulate descriptive feedback using the guidelines suggested in this chapter.

- Invest the time and effort into developing the potential of others consistently and not just on achieving the results required today. **Try this:** Work on understanding what each of your people needs, and help them create specific development plans to improve their effectiveness.

- Do you want more tips and tools? **Try this:** Bookmark our website www.adeptleadership.com/tools-and-tips-adept-booksite/ to access a growing repository of valuable resources.

Chapter 8 – Inspiration

Making Changes that Last

This chapter will use three methods that enable lasting change: Repetition - summarizing the main concepts of the book in the first few pages; Alignment - aligning with practices that are relatable to your experience by sharing some of our clients' real-life scenarios; and Inspiration - the engine of lasting change.

Simple, Not Easy

The power of incremental improvement is truly undeniable. It builds sustainable growth to improve performance and effectiveness. Once we commit to it, we realize that it works in its simplicity of small wins over time. Keep in mind that although it's simple, it is not easy. Frequently when things aren't easy, we try to take shortcuts and talk ourselves into work arounds. We get lazy or bored with the process and anxious for a quicker fix.

The shortcuts sabotage the progress we could have made, so we get frustrated and stop trying. However, if we can stick with it, we can see results and know it will work to help achieve the changes that we want to see or the new habits we want to realize. The other benefit to incremental improvement: it's accessible to a wider range of people.

Think about times where you've seen dramatic growth or substantial changes over a short period. This usually requires lots of untapped talent to make such progress. Incremental implementation is accessible to all.

Plan for Change

Incremental improvement benefits from prior planning. Planning helps set the vision of success based on your core principles and values. In this context, don't think of planning rigidly, like writing a detailed master schedule. Rather, think of planning as simply taking time to crystallize your thoughts. Once you truly clarify your core beliefs and values, it's much easier to set plans and the action steps to move in that direction. It's rare to see progress made incrementally if it's not a planned approach. Without planning, incremental progress is hard to perceive and frustration is easy to focus on. Planning maintains the degree of focus necessary when information overload gets in the way. It allows you to overcome analysis paralysis and realize that some action is necessary to show any progress. Incremental improvement supports progress over perfection and the belief that a B+ in practice is better than an A on the shelf. When your focus is on progress, your attention is easier to manage. You can effectively filter out the overabundance of information that's pulling you off track.

The Fundamentals

A critical step in implementation is simplifying the process you're about to change. Simplification makes it easier to focus and translate data to insight and insight to action. Focus on fundamentals comes into play here. Fundamentals are great because you can check on them quickly in most endeavors. For example, does the salesperson know how to make the ask, does the engineer document their process, and does the operational technician look for the root cause? Once these are evaluated, you can quickly move to higher-level functions. However, if they aren't evaluated early, it can take a long time and a lot of attempts to fix the situation before you realize the problem resides in the implementation of the fundamentals. So, check the fundamentals early and often in any change process.

Insight-Action Loop

/\ —focus (fulcrum)

Because incremental improvement requires action over time, you can benefit from the insight-action loop. As you continually transfer the data you receive into insight, filter that insight into actions that move you in a positive direction. This insight-action loop is critical to progressive improvement as the insight informs you of new actions that need to be taken and the outcomes of those actions provide you with additional insight.

Focus is crucial as you make progress incrementally. It truly is the fulcrum of execution, the leverage point to help you multiply your effort to achieve your objectives. When unfocused, it's easier to be thrown off by obstacles and barriers. It's easy to become distracted and lose a sense of the benefits of doing the work to reach your objectives. With focus, these influences seem to be stripped away and you significantly reduce the effort required to achieve your goals.

Your Attitude

Our attitudes have a huge impact on how we achieve things incrementally. As a habit of thought, how we think will impact the choices we make and the actions we take to achieve the outcomes we want. Although they are molded over time through our background and experience, they can also change incrementally through our focus on our aspirations and objectives and on actions taken in moving in that direction. A critical component in making essential changes in the way we think and act is in our level of awareness. Sometimes we may have blind spots about beliefs or values that are holding us back. We may need to become informed about those things by some outside means.

Our attitudes have a big impact on how we lead. If you believe that to do something right, you have to do it yourself, then you have an attitude that must change in order to become an effective leader. Leaders need to work through and with people, and most can benefit by shoring up the fundamentals of leadership before focusing on more nuanced approaches. As the leader, you are taking care of yourself first and have an idea of your strengths and challenges. You know the path to improvement and are disciplined to act to make improvements. You have a way of creating that same level of discipline or devotion in those that you influence. As a key component of any new initiative, you work at getting others to participate in things that they need to change in the organization.

Discipline as Devotion

Discipline doesn't always mean regimentation. As long as you maintain focus and act on those things that are truly important to you, you can achieve your objectives through unregimented discipline. This allows you to delay gratification and is an outcome of focus and a source of achievement that has been proven to work.

Leaders must be disciplined to achieve organizational goals. Clearly communicating organizational core ideology and values and then living those values helps employees feel good about moving in that direction. Remembering to engage people early and often in the change process builds deep commitment and desire to make the change happen.

To achieve attention management, Primary Focus Areas help us work on those areas that are important but just not urgent. They help us filter out distractions and put our time into the activities that return the biggest bang for the buck.

Being or becoming more authentic builds trust and deepens relationships. It creates a climate in which people are motivated to achieve, rather than having to be coerced through fear and managed with incentives. You can lead through your own style if you forget about the myths of leadership (like leaders are born and not made) and focus instead on the tells of success, those principles we know to work regardless of time or circumstance.

Leadership Is Influence

You don't have to be a formal leader to lead. If leadership is influence, you can lead from any level as long as you positively impact others to accomplish what needs to get done and do it in a way that keeps people engaged and wanting more.

In building teams, share information broadly and encourage people to participate in decisions and solving problems, contributing to team goals, reducing obstacles to completing work, and defining the meaning or larger purpose of the work or the job at hand. As the leader, you must help define objectives and goals and provide critical feedback when goals are met or missed.

Ultimately, your success as the leader can be measured by your ability to reproduce the results you've achieved through other people. Building a bench of people who could replace you helps you move toward sustainability and is a measure of your organizational legacy.

Taking Action

So, how does all this work for <u>YOU</u>?

The following three scenarios give you specific ideas and actions for implementing this incremental discipline in your life. These scenarios are a compilation of real situations with our clients and the actions they have implemented.

Scenario One: Marketing Associate

You are part of a high-functioning marketing team. You've been on the team for three years and feel like you are beginning to hit your stride. Of the nine other team members, you feel you are one of the top performers and you've become intrigued by the possibility that your manager may be looking for their replacement in the very near future.

Awareness

Taking an ADEPT view of your work, you rethink how you're approaching your job. You read more books and watch videos and attend talks about leadership and management. You expose yourself to other people's viewpoints about how they accomplish their work. You become aware that <u>your attitude gets</u> in the way of how your day unfolds. Instead of totally reacting based on what you perceive to be others' intention, you ask more questions to clarify the nature and urgency of their requests. You take a personality profile test that makes you aware of your <u>communication strengths and weaknesses</u>, and you work on improving those. You seek feedback from your peers about your work performance.

Direction

You start to learn how to filter your responsibilities through your boss's perspective and become proactive about setting time up to communicate and interact with her, rather than waiting for her to set time for you. Your workload is focused on those things that you need to accomplish first based on predetermined priorities rather than whatever happens to hit your desk. You also start being proactive about meeting with your peers to talk about your overall goals and to build relationships. At home, you begin to carve out time for yourself to work on projects and focus on intentionally taking time for yourself and for your family.

Execution

important -v- urgent

You begin to use a "chat" sheet by listing items and issues that you need to speak with your boss about as they come to you during the day. You bring them up all at once when you meet, rather than interrupting her frequently throughout the day. You learn that not all emails are important, although they all seem to be urgent. You discuss this with your boss and realize that when she sends you an email at night, she doesn't expect you to act on it right away. She's just catching up on her work when her kids have gone to bed. You realize that you don't need to respond to every email as soon as you get it, and you set up times to check them during the day. As you implement these new habits, you realize that your days are filled with the same tasks, but the way you go through your day is much more satisfying and you have a greater sense of accomplishment.

People-Centric Attitudes

Your increased awareness has helped you realize your colleagues are all different. For the first time, you begin to appreciate those differences and understand that you can rely on different people to do different things more effectively. You try to pick out their unique communication styles, and when working with them, flex your style to see if your communication and relationships improve. In working with two of your colleagues, you see slow but steady improvement with them, and all projects working with them seem to run much smoother.

Talent Management

You realize that you are responsible for your own career growth and development. Working with your supervisor and the feedback you've received, you develop an action plan to work on your career opportunities. You persuade your supervisor to provide you with a detailed overview of the areas you need to work on to take your performance to the next level. You also engage in a couple of professional associations outside of your business to get a perspective on the marketplace and understand how your talents relate to others of comparable background and experience.

* * *

Scenario Two: CEO & Owner

You are the CEO of a plumbing company with one hundred employees. You do residential and commercial projects, and your business is doing well in the city in which you live. You've been in business for ten years - enough to make a go of it and become firmly established - but you still face stiff competition in the marketplace and challenging decisions every day, strategically and tactically.

Awareness

After years of work and achieving a certain level of success, you realize you might have created a prison of your own actions. Whenever you want to step away, you experience tremendous anxiety. When you get back to work, you realize there's been degradation in productivity and quality. You realize that it's not because you've cracked the whip or that people are operating in fear when you are around. It's more that they rely on you, that they literally need you to get some things done and to move the ball forward. You realize that as long as you are in the center of the hub, things will never change. You begin looking for external feedback and support to make the necessary changes.

First, you conduct a 360-degree feedback on yourself. The report reinforces what you suspected: although people are extremely loyal to you and love working for you, they feel as though your hands are in too many pots. You understand that you've created this dilemma, which was fueled when you first started the business driven by your ego. Back then, you wanted to be the one who solved all the problems and made all the decisions. You realize that much of your personal satisfaction has changed. Now, it comes from spending time with family and pursuits to give back to the community out of the office.

Direction

At that moment, you set a new course for your life and quickly begin to implement that into how your business works and how you will manage it. You begin by gathering your senior staff to discuss your personal objectives and share how you need their help to get there. You lay out your plans for your life and your ideas about how it will work with the company. You speak with conviction and clarity and make sure they fully understand *their* focus. Then you encourage them to think about what you've said and come back in a week with some ideas about organizational changes that need to happen to achieve the objective. You indicate that everything is on the table and emphasize that it's okay if any suggestions include changes you need to work on personally.

Execution

You also consult people in your key professional relationships on their perspectives about how you can get it all done. You get great ideas, a few of which you would have never considered on your own. You select one peer to be a sounding board, someone who has a vested interest in you but is removed from the situation so they aren't impacted by the day-to-day interests or long-term emotional impact. You create a template for what an ideal work week looks like, including time to train and coach your senior leaders, time to introduce some of the people in your firm to your key business relationships, and time to focus on your outside-of-work pursuits. You share the plan with an assistant to help keep you on track.

People-Centric Mindset

You take the time to become hyperaware of your senior leadership team. You focus on getting to know them all better, and you begin to understand that they are all motivated differently. You realize that what you've done intuitively and unintentionally has created a very viable and healthy team. However, you become aware that they collaborate more effectively working with you than with each other on their own. You schedule biweekly meetings to review processes and systems as a group. Your intention is twofold: to work on the business issues and to seek ways to break down those barriers so the team can operate more effectively without you having to facilitate and intervene. Sometimes you excuse yourself from the meeting to allow greater collaboration to happen when you're not in the room.

Talent Management

You move away from the doing and spend all your time with your senior team and other groups throughout the organization. You study them and clarify the nature of their strengths and weaknesses. You devote chunks of time to training and developing them from your perspective. You create more formal and ongoing performance review processes so everyone knows where they stand and is aware of their performance gaps. You also institute tuition reimbursement for employees to seek the education and training they need to take their performance to the next level.

* * *

Scenario Three: Operations Director

You are the director of an operations unit in a huge corporate, multinational operation. You have eight direct reports and are responsible for more than four hundred employees. You've been in the role for four years and love the team you've developed. But resources are always in short supply and the direction of the operation seems to change on a weekly basis

Awareness

Although your responsibilities are in a specific area, the span of influence is much greater. If you could just do the job that you are responsible for, it would be a lot easier. However, weekly if not daily, the corporate office's changing tides of strategies and tactics impact how you run your organization. You're in a fast- paced environment with high demands from internal and external customers and stakeholders. You can barely keep your head above water. Even your email inbox is overwhelming. You seem to be running from pillar to post, never have a sense of accomplishment, and your work hours never seem to end. You conclude that your world lacks structure and discipline. You realize it starts with you.

Direction

You know you've been too reactive to the direction and needs of the corporate office for your team to be productive. You've been around long enough to know what results need to be delivered and decide to discount the corporate noise and do what you know to be effective. You consider moving from managing the group to truly leading it by clarifying the top three crucial elements to your team's success. You meet with your team to review your ideas and get their feedback. You make sure they know that all other outside requests they feel prevent them from accomplishing those three objectives need to be funneled through you.

Execution

You initiate a system of personal planning first thing in the morning as a "meeting with yourself" to pause and reflect on what's most important and to organize your primary tasks, meetings, and discussions for the day. You end your day evaluating what you achieved and plan for the upcoming days. This allows you to leave most of your work at the office and only jump on your tablet at home occasionally for critical issues or during pressing deadlines. You don't do it perfectly to start with because it's a new habit, but your day runs much smoother and you have a greater sense of accomplishment when you do, so it encourages you to stay on the path until it becomes a daily routine.

You act as a filter for requests that come from outside your group and are not in alignment with your top three objectives. You do this to make sure your team can focus on those things that matter most. You also set up biweekly meetings with each of your direct reports to look for teaching moments. You complete ad hoc skip level meetings with different departments so you can keep your finger on the pulse of the entire organization. And you plan quarterly all hands meetings to update the group directly to offset rumors and increase transparency.

People-Centric Mindset

You shift from thinking about all the things that need to be done to how you can encourage, develop, and support others to do all the things that need to be done. You come up with a plan for how this will happen and have a meeting to lay out the broad direction with your team. You encourage them to provide feedback on the plan and give them time to commit to the final plan. You also speak more regularly about the purpose of your work and the value it brings to the corporation and the community at large. Slowly, overtime, you see a significantly higher energy level and greater productivity within your team.

Talent Management

Although your team is high performing, opportunities to get everyone even more engaged exist. You identify the biggest gap as providing and receiving feedback. You've always been good at this, so you begin coaching each of your direct reports on the elements of clear and effective feedback. When you catch them being broad and evaluative, you use that moment to show them how they could have been specific and descriptive. You also make sure your teams provide adequate recognition for a job well done, rather than take it for granted. At the same time, you have a few team members who you need to prod. You are making sure they apply appropriate consequences when performance falls short and take action on nonperformers. You look for obstacles to individual performance and seek to provide greater support or remove the barriers to getting things done.

Although these scenarios might not specifically parallel your circumstance, they address common issues. Apply the tactics that are appropriate for you to see your own performance improvements.

Staying ADEPT

As you're making great progress and improvements, it's always easy to slip back into old habits. I'm often asked how to sustain progress without slipping back into old ways. Consider the following critical factors for staying ADEPT:

1. **Pause and reflect.** This is critical to becoming adept and being focused as you go through your day-to-day activities. When it comes to staying adept, the process remains the same, however the context shifts. At this point you would take a bigger view of what you are trying to accomplish.

   - *Do you have aspirations and objectives that still need to be reached?*

   - *Are you moving toward what your heart tells you to do and not just your head?*

   - *Have your aspirations been broken into bite-sized pieces or goals that can be met?*

   - *Are the goals at cross-purposes with other factors that are impacting you?*

   - *Are you becoming the person you really want to be?*

   - *Are all aspects of your life taken into consideration?*

2. **Ask for feedback.** From your perspective, you may think everything is moving smoothly and operating fine. It's often helpful to seek others' viewpoint to understand how you're showing up to

the outside world. Numerous ways you can do this include having one-on-ones with trusted friends and associates, formal conversations with your boss in which you ask for specific and descriptive feedback, and using assessment tools and instruments.

3. **Focus on your goals and their benefits to you.** It's easy to start getting lazy with setting goals. Making non-SMART statements like "be a better communicator" or "lose some weight" don't give you the necessary focus to overcome your obstacles and narrow the gap. And if you're not making progress, make sure you've taken the time to get crystal clear on the benefits of achieving the objective you've set for yourself. Ask yourself why you really, really, really want this. If you can't answer the question, move in a different direction.

4. **Find someone who gives it to you straight.** Implementing change incrementally can be a great challenge and is often hard to do on your own. Sometimes others can see things that you can't see and encourage you in ways that are positive and unexpected. An outside perspective can also help keep you in check when you get off track. This can be a friend, a spouse, a mentor, coach, or colleague. Just make sure they are interested in you and are committed to your success.

5. **Look for ways to break out of comfort zones.** If you are not making progress, it may be that you are not thinking big enough. Look for the possibility that you are holding yourself back. Consider saying yes to an assignment when your first reaction is to say no. Seek people outside of your usual department or work group to better understand how things work beyond your current frame of reference.

6. **Listen and learn, don't just evaluate and judge.** Most people are paid for their judgment and discernment at work. We all can get caught up in the trap of "we already know, we've already tried

that" type of thinking. To always learn and grow is another key to incremental improvement. It is crucial to energy management to feel as though there is always something to look forward to, something that can be improved, and something to add to your repertoire. How boring would life be if you already knew it all?

7. **Care for yourself physically and mentally.** None of this works if you don't care for the vehicle that makes it happen: you and your well-being. Implement exercise and eating right incrementally, do what you can, and look for ways you can get even better. Take time out and off if you need to rejuvenate. Focus on moderate activities, and try to make changes in the long run.

Da Vinci's Devotion

Many historians refer to Leonardo da Vinci as "the most technically gifted artist that ever walked the earth." His most famous work, and arguably the most popular and valuable painting of all time, the *Mona Lisa*, wasn't even started by the master until he was fifty-one years of age.

In addition to painting, Da Vinci had interests in invention, music, mathematics, engineering, anatomy, and many other subjects. He is sometimes known as the father of paleontology and architecture and is credited with various inventions such as the helicopter and parachute. To capture and understand the world around him, he began drawing when he was young. During his life, he worked on hundreds of drawings, was obsessed with the study of light and movement, and had an intimate knowledge of anatomy. This work had a profound effect, summarized as follows by Jon Brooks in his article on the Comfort Pit website "9 Sketching Exercises Leonardo da Vinci Practices to Achieve Mastery":

"According to Daniel Coyle, the author of *The Talent Code*, when we practice a skill an insulator type substance called myelin thickens around our neural circuitry, which in turn makes us more talented. More Myelin = More Talent. The type of practice one engages in is the determinant of how quickly our myelin sheaths thicken around our neural circuits. Good practice, Coyle explains, must test us and stretch our abilities right up to the edge of frustration. Talent without motivation to ceaselessly improve will never lead to mastery."

So, even though he was thought to be a great genius in many areas, it's safe to say that Da Vinci's success as a painter depended upon his years of study (data), observation (insight), and practice (action). He progressed through years of an insight-action loop as he delved into the studies of people, science, anatomy, and light. This practice impacted his success as much as any other contributing factor. The *Mona Lisa*, started by Da Vinci so late in life, was not so much an object of sudden inspiration as it was a summary of his life and the way he lived it. Practice made perfect.

Can You Do It?

Now, you probably will never paint a *Mona Lisa*. However, if you keep working on what's most important to you, appreciate your gaps, and stay diligent to learn and grow with the experience, you can create a masterpiece in your profession.

Da Vinci had his art and science. What do you have? Do you want to become more productive? Practice ways to manage your priorities and energy. Do you want to become a more inspirational leader? Focus on learning and practicing creating a motivational climate. Do you want to master leading people through change? Devote yourself to understanding change management and how to guide people through it. Be in the game acting rather than just accumulating data and sitting on the sidelines. Being adept is a mindset that starts with living with and loving the gap. By following the insights in this book, and acting on them, becoming adept in your pursuits becomes inevitable. You can achieve more of your true potential and accomplish sustainable, long-lasting results.

True lasting change comes more from the heart than the head. You have to really see yourself in the way you want to be. You have to realize that your past does not have to determine the rest of your life. You can change your circumstance by changing how you think, by being patient with your growth, and by being nonjudgmental about your current state.

Here's the great news about becoming and staying adept: it relies on implementing strategies incrementally. It doesn't rely on drama, or huge gains, or "see the light moments," which are significant but rare. Becoming adept is an everyman process.

After practicing the actions in this book incrementally, you'll find that they've become routine. Soon you'll realize that the changes you've made are sticking and that you too can find accomplishment and success that's not just a one-time thing, but sustainable for a lifetime!

Take action now to improve your business. Access these free leadership tools at http://adeptleadership.com/giveaways-adept-booksite/:

Team Survey

Take a look at how your team is doing in three key areas: Clear Direction, Defined Procedures, and Collaboration. This feedback will provide first steps to improving goal achievement and the effectiveness of your team.

Management Effectiveness Snapshot

A short survey that provides a quick snapshot of how you're doing in approaching your role and achieving results as a manager

* * *

If you enjoyed this book, please write a short review (even a sentence helps!). You'll not only help others receive the benefits you've just enjoyed, but it will help me, too. Book rank is highly affected by reviews, so those couple of minutes you'll spend will make a huge difference. Thank you!

71584076R00092

Made in the USA
Middletown, DE
26 April 2018